THE
MITFORD
FAMILY
ALBUM

SOPHIA MURPHY

THE
MITFORD
FAMILY
ALBUM

SIDGWICK & JACKSON
LONDON

First published in Great Britain in 1985
by Sidgwick & Jackson Limited

Copyright © 1985 Sophia Murphy

Book design by James Campus

ISBN 0–283–99115–1

Phototypeset by Falcon Graphic Art Ltd
Wallington, Surrey
Printed in Great Britain by
R. J. Acford, Industrial Estate, Chichester, Sussex
for Sidgwick & Jackson Limited
1 Tavistock Chambers, Bloomsbury Way
London WC1A 2SG

To Anthony & Carole Bamford

I would like to express my warmest thanks to those who have given me invaluable help in writing this book, especially my mother, Deborah Devonshire, and my aunts, Diana Mosley, Pamela Jackson and Jessica Treuhaft.

I am also extremely grateful to Anita Leslie, Jonathan Guinness, Mrs Paul Rodzianko, Mrs Midi Gascoigne, Tim Bailey, Erskine Guinness, my editor, Margaret Willes, and finally my long-suffering landlady and friend, Camilla Scott.

The photographs have come mostly from the family albums of 1st Lord Redesdale, Lady Redesdale, Nancy, Pamela, Diana, Unity and Deborah. I am most grateful to my aunts and my mother for allowing me such generous access. I would also like to thank the Courtauld Institute for the photograph of the Carrington window at Biddesden, the National Monuments Record for Biddesden and Wootton Lodge, the *Illustrated London News* Picture Library for the photograph of Cecil Beaton with Tilly Losch and John Sutro, the Radio Times Picture Library for the picture of Diana at the Union rally in 1948, Hamish Hamilton Limited for the covers of *Noblesse Oblige* and *The Pursuit of Love*, and Sir Geoffrey Shakerley for the portraits of Diana, Pamela and Deborah taken in 1985. The two pictures of Jessica and Esmond Romilly were taken from Philip Toynbee's *Friends Apart*, published by Sidgwick & Jackson.

I am grateful to the following for passages that I have quoted: Diana Mosley's autobiography, *A Life of Contrasts*, published by Hamish Hamilton, 1977; Nancy Mitford's *The Pursuit of Love*, published by Hamish Hamilton, 1949; Peter Quennell's *The Marble Foot*, published by Collins, 1976; and Jessica Mitford's *Hons and Rebels*, published by Victor Gollancz, 1960.

My interest in the Mitford family first began when I was a child. The albums at home were full of photographs and press cuttings of my mother's and aunts' goings on. People used to say to me, 'Oh yes, well of course your mother was a Mitford, what a fascinating family . . .'. I found it very hard to identify these legendary characters, apparently so famous, with my aunts who seemed to me to be perfectly ordinary people. However, I was very fond of them, and greatly looked forward either to their coming to stay, or visits to their houses.

Diana, or 'Honks' as my mother calls her, personified for me the ideal 'grown-up'. She was beautiful, she was always interested in what I had to say, and never said 'run along'. Above all she was never cross, although on several occasions I must have severely tested her patience.

An incident that springs to mind illustrating her tolerance of childish misdemeanours took place when I was about five or six. My mother took me to stay with Diana at her house in France. We went on a shopping expedition, and during one particularly long wait in a shop while my mother tried on clothes, I alleviated my boredom by attempting to wrench the arm off a dummy model in the window. The *vendeuses* were furious and my embarrassed mother was not too pleased, but Diana merely roared with laughter.

Nancy I remember less well. Her jokes were generally too sophisticated to make much impression on a young mind, though she had one particular tease which was very convincing. I had a playmate called James, and Aunt Nancy told me that James was going to accompany her back to Paris after her visit to England. My friend denied this, but when postcards began to arrive from Paris from 'James' I began to believe it, and it was many months before I could be persuaded that Aunt Nancy was 'having me on'.

Aunt Jessica's visits were rare, as she lived in America. She, like Diana, was in no way a typical 'grown-up'. She never talked down to me, but listened seriously to my opinions and, better still, laughed at my jokes, instead of the usual reaction of 'don't be so silly'.

As she lived in England, Pam was the aunt of whom I saw the most. She shares my mother's love of animals and food, and each visit still involves the two sisters comparing notes about their various animals and pets, and endless discussions about recipes. With all the sisters, reminiscing plays a part in every conversation. Almost any subject under discussion would remind one of them of something that had happened in the past, which would be recounted with shrieks of laughter. Typical family life, one might say, which, as a child, is what I thought it was. It was only as I grew older and discovered more, and read and loved their books, that I realized that they were indeed exceptional.

There has already been much written about the Mitfords, both by themselves and by others. Nancy immortalized her family and childhood in her novels, *The Pursuit of Love* and *Love in a Cold Climate*. After she died, Harold Acton wrote a memoir of her life. Diana had her autobiography, *A Life of Contrasts*, published in 1977. Jessica has written two volumes of autobiography, *Hons and Rebels*, and *A Fine Old Conflict*. Deborah is the author of a book on the history of Chatsworth and her experiences in the house, where she now lives as the Duchess of Devonshire. All these books proved to be bestsellers, which indicates great public interest in the family.

What then is the fascination of the Mitfords?

One reason is that their actions when young were considered very outrageous, and were always accompanied by much publicity. In the 1920s and 30s young people were more obedient to parental wishes, and strict protocol helped to control behaviour. For so many children from one family to flaunt so flagrantly authority and to act just as they pleased in so many different ways set new precedents. Everyone has day dreams, but the Mitfords turned theirs into reality.

Secondly, the family knew an extraordinarily eclectic range of people. If the question was asked what do the following people all have in common:

Adolf Hitler
Lytton Strachey
Winston Churchill
Prince Aly Khan
The Duke and Duchess of Windsor
Evelyn Waugh
Hardie Ames
Eric Pountain, the chairman of Tarmac

one answer could be that they were, or are, friends of one or more of the Mitfords.

It is unusual to find so much talent in one family. For four children from a family of seven to have written bestsellers is probably unique. Amongst them, moreover, they have covered a diversity of subjects. Apart from her novels, Nancy was an accomplished historical biographer, writing lives of Louis XIV, Frederick the Great and Madame de Pompadour among others. Jessica has produced fascinating exposures on American prisons and the funeral parlour business. Diana has written a biography of the Duchess of Windsor and, more recently, *Loved Ones*, a series of pen portraits of various friends.

The pictorial material for this book comes largely from the sisters' photograph albums. My task was much facilitated by the fact that the albums are mostly meticulously labelled with names, dates and places.

Diana's books are fascinating. The chronology is often mixed up. Thus on one page there might be a drawing by Helleu of Lady Redesdale as a child in the 1890s, next to a pixture of a picnic with the Mitfords' cousins, Winston Churchill and his children, which in turn is beside a photograph of Diana with Hitler and other Third Reich leaders, having tea together. The album looks, at first glance, like any other photograph book, but a closer inspection reveals an extraordinarily varied collection of people all incongruously jumbled up together, as it is very unlikely that they would have been in such close juxtaposition in real life.

Like Diana, Debo has never bothered too much with exact chronology in her albums, and she does not limit hers to photographs of her friends and family. The books also reflect her changing interests over the years. In a post-war album there is a large picture of Marilyn Monroe, and another of the jockey, Gordon Richards, cut out of magazines. Debo's most recent book also contains newspaper cuttings, but these are articles about Tarmac, the building firm of which she is a director, or about the garden furniture business that she has set up at Chatsworth.

Unity's albums give a thorough pictorial account of her life up to 1939. Many pages have drawings and illuminations, showing an artistic talent which she never really fulfilled. There are several books filled with photographs of her life in Germany. These, all neatly captioned in German, are a fascinating documentation of the 'informal' side of Nazi Germany, showing many of the leaders away from their official roles.

Pamela's albums are typical of her, in that she gives equal priority to photos of her animals as to her friends and relations. Nancy did the same in her early albums, which contain almost exclusively pictures of her horses and family, giving no indication of her later sophistication.

It was thanks to these albums that I was able to put together this compilation of family photographs. The family came into existence as the result of the union of Sydney Bowles and David Freeman Mitford. Sydney was the daughter of Thomas Gibson Bowles, a highly eccentric character who, after his wife's early death, tried to get over his loss by lengthy sea voyages. He took his children with him, and so much of their teenage years were spent aboard his yacht and visiting foreign countries. He founded the magazine, *Vanity Fair*, and then launched *The Lady*, which is still going to this day.

David Freeman Mitford was the second son of Algernon Bertram, 1st Lord Redesdale. Like Thomas Bowles, 'Bertie' was an adventurer, and spent many years in the Fat East as a diplomat. He explored Japan, then rarely visited by Westerners, and mastered enough of the language to translate several books of Japanese legends into English, including the classic *Tales of Old Japan*.

Sydney and David were married in February 1904, and wasted no time in starting a family. In November that year Nancy was born. She was followed by Pamela in 1907, Tom in 1909, Diana in 1910, Unity in 1914, Jessica in 1917 and Deborah in 1920. Their upbringing was, by today's standards, unusual – though there must be many eccentric parents whose idiosyncracies, through lack of any literary children, have never been recorded.

Lord Redesdale did not believe in education for girls, and only Tom, who was sent to Eton, received any sort of conventional education. The girls were taught at home by a series of governesses, few of whom stayed long, as they were quite unable to cope with the mutinous behaviour which ensued if any attempts were made to impose discipline. Not all the governesses were unpopular; one taught her charges shop-lifting, another spent all day playing racing demon with them.

This school-room education was received with varying enthusiasm from the sisters. Nancy and Jessica longed to go to school, while the thought of being sent away filled Pamela, Diana and Debo with dread. Unity managed to persuade her parents to send her to boarding school, but after she had been expelled from three different ones, they gave up. Deborah went for three days, but she was so unhappy that she was removed.

So, apart from very half-hearted attempts to educate them, the sisters had to rely on each other and their own resources for occupation.

David Mitford succeeded to the title of Lord Redesdale in 1916, his elder brother having been killed in action in 1915. He inherited Batsford, a large Tudor-style house built in Gloucestershire by his father. It was expensive to run, and when the war was over it was sold and the family moved to Asthall Manor in Oxfordshire. The older children loved this house. A barn was converted to a library where the children were left to themselves, and where they could read and Tom could play the piano.

Lord Redesdale did not, however, plan to stay indefinitely at Asthall. With part of the proceeds from the sale of Batsford, he began building a house on the site of a farm near Swinbrook, three miles away. The family moved there in 1927, acquiring at the same time a house in London, in Rutland Gate.

The new house at Swinbrook was stark and plain, but Lord Redesdale, who had supervised its building, was not concerned with architectural beauty. His idea was to build a house large enough for his family; a roof under which they could eat and sleep whilst getting on with more important activities which all took place out of doors.

Like Lord Redesdale's views on education, the new house was received by his children with varying degrees of delight or displeasure. Nancy, Tom and Diana objected to its ugliness, and mourned the loss of the library at Asthall, for at Swinbrook there was no room apart from the nursery set aside for the children. Jessica, having no love for hunting, found the winters in the country especially oppressive and interminable. Pamela and Debo, however, were completely happy. They both loved animals and country life, and so their lives at Swinbrook were contented and fulfilled, although Pamela did not live there for long.

Lord Redesdale was a man of violent likes and dislikes. Under the heading of dislikes came most of the county neighbours, whose children, as a result, were not encouraged as playmates. As the older children grew up constant battles were fought with their father to be allowed to have their friends to stay, especially those men friends of Diana and Nancy whom he considered namby-pamby aesthetes. But to give a picture of him as a cruel tyrant would be quite false. His children adored him, and he them, and to those outsiders whom he liked, he was enormously charming and kind.

Money was a constant worry to Lord and Lady Redesdale. It was not a subject ever discussed, so no one knew exactly what had happened to the fortune left by 1st Lord Redesdale in 1916, except that it had been much reduced. To economize, David let Rutland Gate and Swinbrook from time to time, and took his family to live at the Old Mill Cottage in High Wycombe, which had been bought by Sydney's father at the time of her marriage.

By 1935 Lord Redesdale could no longer afford to keep Swinbrook with all the expenses of a large estate, and so it was sold, the Old Mill Cottage becoming the Mitfords' permanent home.

The older children did not regret the move – anyway, they were grown up and were leading their own lives. Deborah, however, minded dreadfully leaving Swinbrook, and it was many years before she could bring herself to return. But earlier life at Asthall and Swinbrook was not forgotten, and wonderful descriptions of family life there were reproduced in Nancy's novel, *The Pursuit of Love*.

From the time that she first came out in 1922, Nancy was popular and much in demand. Brian Howard (the character on whom Anthony Blanche in *Brideshead Revisited* was partly based) described her to Harold Acton as 'a delicious creature, quite pyrotechnical, my dear, and sometimes even profound, and would you believe it, she's hidden away among the cabbages of the Cotswolds'.

By the time she was twenty-eight, Nancy had had two novels published, *Highland Fling* and *Christmas Pudding*. These, although not of the calibre of her post-war novels, are light-hearted and amusing, portraying exactly the attitudes and reproducing the language of the Bright Young Things of the 1920s.

When Nancy was twenty-three she became unofficially engaged to Hamish St Clair Erskine, and this unsatisfactory relationship continued for five years. Hamish was four years younger and, although undoubtedly very fond of Nancy, he dilly-dallied and vacillated about actually getting married, and finally the affair petered out. Soon after this, Nancy fell in love with Peter Rodd, the son of the British Ambassador to Rome, Lord Rennell, and they were married a few months later at the end of 1933. But sadly the marriage was never really a success. Peter Rodd, although charming and handsome, was a spineless individual. He had very little money, but was unable to keep a job for more than a few weeks. He had none of Nancy's strength of mind and discipline, and was also notoriously unfaithful to her. Nancy had to work hard to support them both, and it was not long before his cavalier attitude, once so attractive, began to lose its charm. By the end of the war the marriage had fizzled out (though they were not divorced until 1958) and Nancy settled for good in Paris. It was here that she enjoyed real success as a writer with her novels and historical biographies, and where finally she found happiness in a love affair with France which lasted until she died.

Pamela and Tom, born three and five years after Nancy, are the two Mitfords about whom least has been written. Pamela always loved the country, and after Diana and Bryan Guinness went to live at Biddesden in Hampshire, she went there to manage their farm. In 1936 she married Derek Jackson, a brilliant physicist who held the chair of spectroscopy at Oxford.

Apart from being clever, he was amusing and brave, and cared not a hoot for so-called conventions or authority.

Pamela and her husband lived first at Rignell House, near Oxford, and then in County Tipperary. But soon after they separated in 1951 she returned to England and bought a house in Gloucestershire where she has lived ever since. She loved and was loved by all her sisters, and has never allowed politics to come between her and other members of her family.

Tom, perhaps the cleverest of all the children, never had the opportunity to fulfil his expectations. He was very musical, to the extent that he spent time studying music in Vienna before deciding instead to become a barrister. This was an apt choice as he loved arguing, and used to pay his sisters by the hour to argue with him. But he had not been qualified long when the war came. He immediately joined up, and was killed in Burma in April 1945. He is summed up by Diana in her autobiography: 'A day never passes when I do not think of him and mourn my loss. He was clever, wise and beautiful; he loved women, and music and his family.'

Diana was the nearest to Tom in age, only a year younger, and it seems every good fairy was at her birth. Not only is she the most beautiful of the sisters, but very clever and loved by everyone who knew or knows her. When she was eighteen she married Bryan Guinness, and they were regarded as the quintessential glamorous couple – a view quickly adopted by the press. Their friends were all the most attractive and intelligent people – Lytton Strachey, Lord Berners and Evelyn Waugh amongst others.

However, when Diana met Sir Oswald Mosley in 1932, she was at once spellbound by him. He was at this time already married with a family, and very busy in politics, so he and Diana could only snatch odd moments together. She loved him so much that she was prepared to accept this way of life. But, in 1933 Sir Oswald's wife, Cimmie, died of peritonitis, and in 1936 he and Diana were secretly married. Thus began the forty-four years they were together; years which held a vast range of experiences, like the horror of their imprisonment during the war, the loss by fire of their beloved house in Ireland, the joy brought by the birth of two sons, but, above all, the complete and unwavering love and happiness that they found in each other.

It is always sad when politics cause a rift in a once close-knit family, but unfortunately the right-wing opinions of Diana and Unity and the left-wing views of Jessica became too extreme to be reconcileable. Jessica was aware from an early age that she wanted a different sort of life from that of her upbringing. Aged twelve, she opened a 'running-away account', in which she invested every spare penny to be saved for when the opportunity to escape finally presented itself. She, like Nancy, complained of the tedium of life at home, and it is to their great credit as writers that, on reading the fascinating and hilarious accounts of their childhood, tedium is the last emotion to spring to mind. Jessica and Unity's differing political views began almost as a joke when they were teenagers. If Unity was going to be a Fascist, then she, Jessica, would be a Communist. Determined to learn more on the subject, Jessica spent some of her precious running-away money on left-wing literature, and on studying it she realized she genuinely and seriously believed in its tenets.

True to her word as a child, she did run away. When she was nineteen, in 1937, she met Esmond Romilly, a Communist since his school days. He had gone to Spain to fight for the Republicans in the Civil War, and so was a hero in Jessica's eyes. Her feelings for him were reciprocated and, after executing a well-thought-out plan to hoodwink the Redesdales, they ran away together. Attempts were made by the Redesdales to get them back, but to no avail, and they were married in France shortly afterwards.

The Romillys moved to America in 1939, where a daughter, Constancia, was born. When Germany invaded Russia, Esmond joined up, and he was killed in action in 1941. Jessica remained in America, and in 1943 she married Robert Treuhaft, a lawyer of left-wing sympathies. Now, she and her husband live in Oakland, California, where she has enjoyed great success with books and journalism.

I do not have the space in this short introduction to redress the inaccuracies and myths that have arisen about Unity. I will go into those in more detail in the book itself. Politics caused an irreparable rift between herself and Jessica but, until then, they had been the best of friends. Unity was much loved by her other sisters for her bright, bold character, her eccentricity, and her bravery. Diana describes her in her autobiography: 'Unity had all the qualities that Muv [Lady Redesdale] most admired: fearlessness, generosity, independence, a total absence of deviousness.' Her attempted suicide in Germany at the outbreak of war, and her twilight existence until her death in 1948 was, for her friends and family, a very great tragedy.

Deborah, the youngest, grew up amongst all the drama of her sisters' much-publicised activities. However, she had an exceptionally happy childhood, and got on with her life despite the storms around her.

In 1941 she married Lord Andrew Cavendish, who, because his elder brother was killed in action during the war, became the 11th Duke of Devonshire on the death of his father in 1950.

Deborah's sisters used to tease her for her lack of intellectual pursuits – Nancy called her '9' because, she said, she had a mental age of nine and was unable to read. This is another of the myths that grew up in the family. Deborah is an extremely well-read and intelligent woman, which was proved by the great success of her book abut Chatsworth, *The House*.

After the war Deborah and Andrew led a glamorous life, spending much of their time doing what would now be called jet-setting. But, when they moved to Chatsworth in 1959 they had to face the huge responsibilities of running their vast estates. Deborah spends virtually all her time in the country, where she is at her happiest, as she was as a child at Swinbrook.

These, then, are the chief characters who will appear in the pages of this family album.

Sophia Murphy

June 1985

'The Light of Asia', statue of Japanese Buddha in the garden at Batsford

Algernon Mitford, always known as Bertie, was born in London in 1837. He was educated at Eton (where he was a close friend of his cousin Algernon Swinburne) and Oxford, and on leaving university he joined the Foreign Office. His first appointment was to St Petersburg in 1863 but in 1865 he volunteered for and secured a post in Peking. This marked the beginning of a lifelong fascination and love for the East. In 1866 he was transferred to Japan where, apart from conducting a most distinguished diplomatic career, he became accomplished enough in the Japanese language to translate into English *Tales of Old Japan*. When it was published by Macmillan in London it immediately became a bestseller.

Bertie returned to England in 1874. The Prime Minister, Benjamin Disraeli, who had some years before spotted him as a bright young man, appointed him secretary to the Board of Works. In this capacity he was responsible for, among other things, maintaining the royal residences, government buildings and the royal parks. He threw himself into this work with enthusiasm, restoring Hampton Court, organizing a large amount of rebuilding at the Tower of London and renovating sections of Windsor Castle. The London parks were virtually re-landscaped to his design; out of briar-and-weed-filled wildernesses he created attractive and well-stocked gardens.

Shortly after his appointment to the Board of Works, Bertie married Lady Clementine Ogilvy, second daughter of the Earl of Airlie. She was twenty-one, he thirty-seven, but the age gap did not prevent them from enjoying a particularly happy marriage. Over the next twenty years Bertie and Clementine had nine children of whom David Mitford was the third, born in 1878. They lived in Chelsea, where they were friends with neighbours such as James McNeill Whistler and Thomas Carlyle. Bertie commissioned Whistler to paint Clementine's portrait but, just as it was nearly finished, Whistler ripped it into shreds rather than have it seized by pursuing creditors.

In 1886 Bertie inherited Batsford, the family estate in Gloucestershire. Wasting no time, he pulled down the existing Georgian house, Georgian architecture being anathema to him, and built another one, bigger and better, in mock Elizabethan style. Then, using his experience gained from looking after the royal parks, he set about creating a garden. This garden with its arboretum of thousands of species of trees is still in existence, and flourishes under the care of its present owner, Lord Dulverton.

Right Algernon Bertram Freeman Mitford, 1st Baron Redesdale of the second creation, 1837–1916

Bertie Mitford commissioned the firm of architects
Sir Ernest George & Peto to build a large house in
the Cotswold Elizabethan style, with buttresses,
castellated bay windows, a gabled porch and other
embellishments so beloved by the Victorians.

Batsford Park, near Moreton-in-Marsh, Gloucestershire

Thomas Gibson Bowles was born in 1841, the illegitimate son of Thomas Milner Gibson, a Suffolk land-owner and MP. His mother's identity is unknown, but from the age of three he was brought up by his father and step-mother.

After a short spell as a clerk at Somerset House, which he did not enjoy, he decided to pursue a career in journalism. He had often contributed to newspapers and magazines, writing articles in his spare time, but now he decided to go further and start his own magazine. Thus, *Vanity Fair* was launched in 1868. The magazine, containing political articles, literary criticism and society news, started to do well when Bowles introduced the now famous *Spy* cartoons. Each week a well-known figure was depicted with an accompanying description. Some years later, in 1885, he started the *Lady* magazine which is still going today.

In 1876 Thomas Bowles married Jessica Evans Gordon, the daughter of a major-general from Southampton. By 1885 they had four children; two girls and two boys, of whom Sydney, the future Lady Redesdale, was the third. A couple of years later Jessica was again expecting a baby, but complications arose which proved fatal, and she died leaving an absolutely devastated Thomas to bring up four small children. This responsibility he undertook with devotion, though he did have some unusual ideas for those days on the subject of upbringing. For example, the children were raised on a kosher diet, and were not permitted any shellfish, rabbit or pork (rules which Lady Redesdale was later to apply to her children). Medicine was another forbidden commodity. Thomas considered the body would recover itself far quicker if left alone than if tampered with by doctors and their so-called cures.

After the death of his wife, Thomas tried to get over his loss by taking his daughters on a long voyage. He had learnt about boats and sailing as a boy on the Suffolk coast, and was by now a highly competent yachtsman. The voyage was a great success, and he returned in much better spirits. From then on, his yacht, *The Nereid*, and her replacement, *The Hoyden*, played a large part in Thomas's life, and he would invariably spend several months away on a cruise each year.

In 1889 Thomas sold *Vanity Fair*. He had been offered a substantial price for it, and he wanted to concentrate on becoming an MP. He stood as Conservative member for the Norfolk constituency of King's Lynn in the general election of 1892, winning his seat from the Liberals by eleven votes. His career in politics started auspiciously enough, but later he began disagreeing with and voting against his own party to such a degree that in 1904 the Conservatives adopted another candidate for his constituency.

Bowles at work at his desk, 1880

Piqued by this, Thomas switched allegiance to the Liberal Party, continuing to stand in King's Lynn. He returned to Parliament for a short time after the 1910 election, but this marked the end of his time in politics, and he returned to his first love, his boats. He became a master mariner and a much-respected authority on sailing. It was on one of his beloved cruises to Gibraltar in 1921 that he died at the age of eighty.

Left Thomas Gibson Bowles by *Spy*

Ch. Ch. Oxford.
May 22, 1891.

My dear Sydney,

I am so sorry, and so ashamed! Do you know, I didn't even know of your existence? And it was such a surprise to hear that you had sent me your love! It felt just as if Nobody had suddenly run into the room, & had given me a kiss! (That's a thing that happens to me, most days, just now.) If only I had known you were existing, I would have sent you heaps of love, long ago. And, now I come to think about it, I ought to have sent you the love, without being so particular about whether you existed or not. In some ways, you know, people, that don't exist, are much nicer than people that do. For instance people that don't exist are never cross: and they never contradict you: and they never tread on your toes! Oh, they're ever so much nicer than people that do exist! However, never mind: you can't help existing, you know; and I daresay you're just as nice as if you didn't.

Which of my books shall I give you, now that I know you're a real child? Would you like "Alice in Wonderland"? Or "Alice Under Ground"? (That's the book just as I first wrote it, with my own pictures).

Please give my love, and a kiss, to Weenie, and Vera, + yourself (don't forget the kiss to yourself, please: on the forehead is the best place.)
        Your affectionate friend,
        Lewis Carroll.

Sydney Bowles aged eight, in 1888

Although Sydney lost her mother when she was only seven, life with her highly original father was far from dull, and she never suffered the isolated existence of many Victorian children. In 1887 Thomas took his family on a long cruise, and for six months Sydney's home was aboard the 150-foot schooner, *The Nereid*. They visited many countries, starting with the North African coast and then sailing to Alexandria, from which they travelled to Jerusalem and the Holy Land. Sydney loved these adventures and continued to accompany her father on his travels right up to the time of her marriage in 1904.

Amongst Thomas Bowles's many friends was Charles Dodgson, in real life mathematics don at Christchurch College, Oxford, but better known to posterity as Lewis Carroll, author of *Alice in Wonderland* and *Alice Through the Looking Glass*. The letter opposite was enclosed in a copy of *Alice's Adventures Underground*, the original title of *Alice in Wonderland*, which Dodgson sent as a present to Sydney.

Left Letter to Sydney Bowles from Lewis Carroll (the Rev. Charles Lutwidge Dodgson)

David Mitford in his uniform prior to setting off for South Africa,
February 1900

David Mitford always liked the idea of the army, and the outbreak of the Boer War in 1899 enabled him to join up with the Northumberland Fusiliers and to fight. The following June he was taken prisoner by the Boers, though his letter home to his father, posted by General Smuts, makes clear that he was not badly treated. However, he derived particular satisfaction later from escaping.

Towards the end of 1900 a serious chest wound, as a result of which he lost a lung, caused him to be invalided out of the army and he was never again passed fit for active service. He was lucky to survive the wound, as he had lain in an ox-cart in the cruel African heat for two days before receiving treatment. But he had an incredibly strong constitution which was further tested by the fact that, although he had only one lung, he smoked sixty cigarettes a day and lived to the age of eighty.

POST OFFICE TELEGRAPHS.

No. of Telegram......

If the accuracy of an Inland Telegram be doubted, the telegram will be repeated on payment of half the amount originally paid for its transmission, any fraction of 1d. less than ½d. being reckoned as ½d.; and if it be found that there was any inaccuracy, the amount paid for repetition will be refunded. Special conditions are applicable to the repetition of Foreign Telegrams.

Charges to pay

£ s. d.

Handed in at — War Office London — at 12.55 p.m. — Received here at 1.12 p.m.

TO — Freeman Mitford C.B. Batsford Park - Moreton in Marsh

Following telegram just received from South Africa begins referring to your telegram 3223 of 20 July David Mitford and Hon. John Marsham 40th Company Imperial Yeomanry were taken prisoners 7

N.B.—This Form must accompany any Inquiry made respecting this Telegram.

June David Mitford has since escaped and reported personally to Base depot enquiry being made respecting Marsham ends Fleetwood Wilson War Office

N.B.—This Form must accompany any Inquiry made respecting this Telegram.

War Office's telegram announcing David's capture by the Boers, June 1900

COPY

LETTER POSTED
BY
GENERAL SMUTS

Made prisoner this 7th June 1900

My dear Father

I am allowed to write you a line by kind permission from the Commandant. I am a prisoner but unhurt. I shall be able to tell you all some other day.
Please let my great friend's people know he is also unhurt

but a prisoner, his people's address Kettering and his name is Hon. John Marsham we are great friends and shall stick together.
Cheer mother up the war will soon be over now.
your very affectionate son
David

David's letter to Lord Redesdale, telling him of his capture

David Mitford in 1902, convalescing from the chest wound received in the Boer War

David and Sydney as Apaches at a fancy dress party in 1906

David and Sydney had known each other since their teens, as their fathers were friends and the Bowles family had stayed at Batsford on several occasions. The young couple were fond of each other, but a serious romance did not become a consideration until David went to fight in South Africa. During his long stay in hospital after being wounded in 1900, he realized that he was in love with Sydney, and there is a story that he dictated a love letter to be sent to her in the event of his death. He returned home in 1901, but it took several months of convalescence before he was well enough to lead an active life. As he recovered, he began paying serious court to Sydney, and in 1903 they became engaged. Their fathers were pleased with the match – though Thomas Bowles was to miss his elder daughter's efficient house-keeping – and Sydney was acquiescent, if not as enthusiastic as her fiancé. Before she was engaged she had been passionately in love with a very attractive flirt called Edward Meade, and many people considered her still to be in love with

him when she accepted David. It was not until after their marriage that she began to reciprocate his feelings. They were married in London in February 1904, and Thomas Bowles lent them his yacht, *The Hoyden*, for a honeymoon cruise.

On their return to London, David went to work for his father-in-law as office manager at the *Lady* magazine. A job in an office was not what he would have chosen ideally; he found life in the city claustrophobic, and was only really happy and fulfilled when working out of doors. But at this time his elder brother Clement was still alive and in those days younger sons were rarely given more than a small allowance, so David was unable to buy a farm or land of his own. However, they were not restricted to spending all the year in London, as Sydney had a small cottage on the outskirts of High Wycombe given to her by her father, and there were frequent visits to David's parents at Batsford.

David and Sydney Mitford soon after their marriage

At the time of her marriage Sydney was a tall, slim girl with blue eyes and light brown hair. Many considered her a beauty and, indeed, by accounts in her diaries, she had plenty of admirers before her engagement to David Mitford. She does not photograph particularly well, as her conspicuously turned-down mouth makes her look too severe and disapproving.

After their marriage, David and Sydney moved into Graham Street in Chelsea, and the photograph on the left was taken at their house there.

On 28 November 1904 Nancy was born. Although they had wanted a boy, they were thrilled with their baby. David wrote enthusiastically to his mother describing the event: 'She [Sydney] is in splendid spirits, I cannot tell you how sweet and brave she has been all through. She wanted a boy, but is very pleased as things are. The baby is splendid, 9½ lbs at birth, and the prettiest child you could see.' David was present at the birth, and there is a story that he administered the anaesthetic himself.

Nancy was very spoilt as a child, largely because David's eldest sister, Frances Kearsey, had a theory that it was very damaging for a child to be spoken to crossly, and that there should 'never be an angry word'. Probably as a result of this, Nancy used to throw tremendous rages, according to Sydney, 'often shaming us in the street'.

Left Sydney Mitford in 1907
Below Nancy on a rocking horse in 1907
Right David and Sydney Mitford with Nancy, aged two, in 1906

'Leag against Nancy' badge
Below Tom and Diana in 1913
Right Pamela in 1913

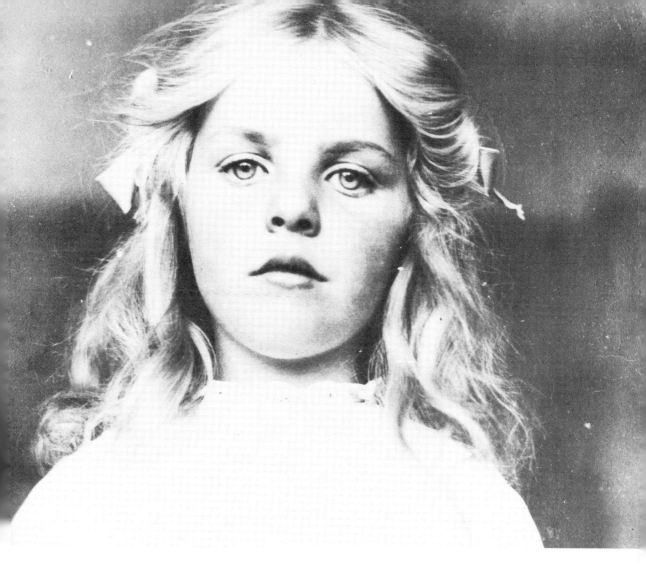

In 1913 the family were based in London, where David Mitford was still working as office manager for the *Lady* magazine. He was competent at this but was never really happy, and longed for a country existence. He did, however, keep a pet mongoose for hunting rats at the office, as a substitute, maybe, for the real thing. His family was increasing. In November 1907, three years after Nancy, Pam was born. Two years later, to Sydney and David's joy, they had a son whom they christened Thomas. Sydney had always wanted boys, and David was delighted to have an heir. In June 1910 she gave birth to another girl, Diana. When she was born the current nanny said to Sydney, 'She's too beautiful, she can't live long.' This prediction nearly came true. When Diana was six she contracted appendicitis and was operated on by the local doctor in one of the guest bedrooms at Batsford. In those days an appendectomy was still a dangerous operation, but

Diana survived, and she says she is sure her recovery was aided by the pretty and comfortable, albeit unhygienic, surroundings of the visitor's room.

Nancy, the eldest, teased her brother and sisters mercilessly. Efforts were sometimes made to organize themselves against her, like Tom's 'Leag against Nancy', but she was too clever for them and her power was never undermined. According to Pam, Nancy

would go on teasing until one cried, and none of us could stop her or outwit her. When we grew up and were coming out, her favourite tease was to find out whoever it was that we fancied – which she always managed to do, whatever our efforts at secrecy – and then tell us that she had seen him at a dance the night before, where he had proposed to her. So convincing was she at this that one almost believed her, even though she did it time and time again and we knew she was teasing.

The Shack, Swastika, Canada

In 1908 David Mitford staked a claim for forty acres in Swastika, Northern Ontario, to speculate for gold. Sir Harry Oakes was to make a fortune on some land adjoining, so it was not a foolish speculation. Unfortunately, although gold in some quantities was found on all the surrounding land, only negligible quantities were found on the Mitford plot.

David and Sydney first visited Swastika in 1913, and it was here that Unity was conceived: an odd irony.

They had planned to make the journey on the *Titanic*, but for some reason they had to change their plans, and instead went out later in the year.

At Swastika they lived in a wooden cabin known as the Shack. This was very basic; all the water had to be pumped by hand, there were no servants and Sydney did all the cooking. The Shack and its forty acres were sold in the 1960s, after the death of Lord Redesdale.

David Mitford at the Shack

No particular news   The Hon Mrs David
likely to stay here   The Hon Mr D.
Moving all the time   Honble Mrs David
Have been in action   Honble Mr D
Not likely write some time   Mrs David
Leaving here soon   Mr D.
We dont know where we are
    going   The Honble Mr David
Have joined regiment   The Honble Mr D
Have joined another regiment   Mrs Mitford
Negative   X before name

We are going towards   Please pay (1st
      3 letters of town)
We are at   Pay (1st 3 letters)

Marching   Tell this to
   North   Nelly
   South   Susan
   East   Emily
   West   Walter

Our War code, addresses on
Letters & Their meanings

David Mitford's war code, sent to his family at the beginning of the First World War

The First World War was to bring tragedy to the Mitford family. David's elder brother, Clement, was killed in action on 13 May 1915. Clement was extraordinarily handsome, much loved and in many ways his parents' favourite. His death not only struck a terrible blow to his family, but also meant that David became Lord Redesdale's heir, and inherited his title and estates the following year.

All Bertie Redesdale's five sons fought in the war, but because of injuries sustained in the Boer War, David was not passed fit for service at the Front. Determined to be of some use to King and Country, however, he rejoined his old regiment, the Northumberland Fusiliers, as Transport Officer. Part of this work involved galloping through Ypres every night, sometimes twice, bringing provisions, ammunition and stores for the men at the Front. He said about his work, 'no one could pretend that the transport ride through Ypres was in the nature of a picnic, but it was of course a very soft job compared with the trenches'. Despite this comment, David often encountered much danger on his journeys, but he never failed to deliver the provisions, and he received a mention in dispatches for his courage.

Right David in uniform during the First World War

Pam and Tom in 1915

Nancy, Tom, Diana and Pam in 1914

Nanny Blor in 1918

At the outbreak of the First World War, David Mitford left immediately with his regiment to fight in France, leaving behind a wife and five children. They lived mostly in their London house in Victoria Road, Kensington, but there were holidays spent at Sydney's cottage in High Wycombe, and at the houses of her father and father-in-law.

Sydney was assisted in looking after her family by a nursery maid and a nanny. The nanny, Laura Dicks, or Blor as she was always known, came to the Mitfords in 1910 and remained with the family until she retired. She was entirely selfless, devoting her life to looking after others, and the children adored her. Although she was never cross, she exerted more control over the children than either of their parents did.

Lady Redesdale was determined that her children, although loved, were certainly not over-indulged, but Tom developed a method for getting things he wanted, which is described by Diana in *A Life of Contrasts*.

We wanted nearly everything; the question was, how to get it if one might not ask. Tom thought of a way round; he called it 'my artful scheme of happiness'. He looked long and lovingly at the desired object, and when this had been noticed he began to speak.

'*Oh what* a lovely box; I don't think I've ever seen such a *lovely* little box in my life. Oh how I wish I could find one like it! Do you think I ever could? *Oh* [to the owner] you are lucky.' He made his voice positively sag with desire. It nearly always ended in his being given whatever it might be he craved. Tom was seven when he invented his artful scheme of happiness.

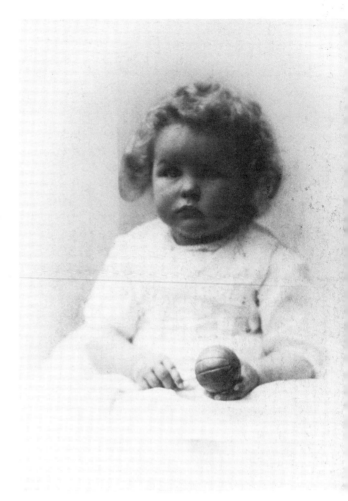

Tom aged nine   Decca aged two

Unity was born on 8 August 1914, shortly after the outbreak of war. Sydney chose the name Unity in the hope that there would soon be peace in Europe, and her father suggested Valkyrie as a second name, after the war maidens of the old Norse legends.

Three years later, on 7 September 1917, Jessica was born at Batsford, and was christened after Sydney's mother. That year Tom went away to his preparatory school, Lockers Park. He was happy at boarding school, popular, good at games and lessons, and already showing a precocious musical talent. He was also possibly quite relieved to be away from the exclusively female household at Batsford, and to have some other little boys to play with.

Left Unity in 1918 aged four

Algernon Bertram Mitford, 1st Lord Redesdale, in his study at Batsford

Bertie Redesdale lived at Batsford until his death in 1916. As Clement, his eldest son, had been killed in France in 1915, David inherited the title, house and land on his father's death. The family, which then consisted of Nancy, Pam, Diana, Tom and Unity, moved in immediately to their new home. Wartime economies restricted them to living in only a few rooms with a skeleton staff, but Sydney eked out their income by having as boarders the children of neighbours in London, Ronald and Lady Florence Norman. All the children got on well together, but Diana remembers being very surprised to see Ronald Norman sitting reading.

'Does your father often read?' she asked Sibell Norman.

'Oh yes,' replied Sibell.

'I've never heard of a *man* reading,' said Diana.

David abhorred the written word. He used to say, 'I read *White Fang*, and it was so frightfully good I've never bothered to read another book.'

Shortly after the family moved to Batsford, Sydney organized a fête in the grounds as a contribution to the war effort. Suddenly she thought the White Elephant stall looked much too bare, so she added to it things from the house, including some of her father-in-law's oriental collection. David, home on leave, and the children managed to buy some back, but many of the valuables fell into other hands.

At Batsford the family used to see a lot of their relations who lived nearby. The children's favourite was Lady Blanche Hozier, known as Aunt Natty, who was Clementine Redesdale's sister. As the young Mitfords considered their parents to be pillars of conventional and respectable behaviour, Aunt Natty's eccentricities, so unusual in a grown-up, made a refreshing change. She never got dressed until lunchtime, but used to walk around the village with a cloak over her nightgown. She used to communicate with her friends by means of long telegrams, an extravagance much disapproved of by the frugal Sydney. The children adored her, and her lack of convention was much respected by them.

Left The Hall and the Library at Batsford

Unity and Decca at Asthall in 1922

Nancy and Debo in 1923

When Debo was born in 1920, Lady Redesdale obviously considered the sixteen-year-old Nancy capable of looking after her in the event of her being orphaned, as she made Nancy a godmother. Debo, when young, must have been grateful that her eldest sister was never called upon to perform these duties, as with her sharp tongue and constant teasing she would have been a severe guardian.

As the three youngest children grew up there were much looked forward to visits from cousins, and neighbourhood children would sometimes come over, but mostly they just had each other for company.

Decca and Unity had a favourite occupation which was their secret language, 'Boudledidge'. It was intelligible only to themselves and therefore proved very useful for singing risqué rhymes and talking to each other in front of the grown-ups.

Decca and Debo started the Society of Hons (Hons here being derived from hens, not from the fact they were honourables). Anyone they disliked was known as a 'Counter Hon', poor Tom frequently being the chief of these.

Debo, being the youngest, was the most teased, but there were dire consequences to be faced for anyone caught making her cry. This was not hard to do. Any sad story, especially one involving animals, resulted in tears welling up in Debo's eyes.

Asthall was the house of the Mitfords from 1919 until 1926. Lord Redesdale never meant this to be the permanent home of his family, as his intention, which he eventually carried out, was to build a house at Swinbrook, the next village. However, the elder children grew up at Asthall and loved it dearly. There was a barn in the garden which Lord Redesdale converted into a library for all the books from Batsford. Being some distance from the house it was ideal for the children as a retreat in which to read or chat, or to listen to Tom playing the piano.

Days followed a regular routine: lessons with the governess from 9.30 a.m. until noon; lunch was at 1.00 p.m.; after lunch, whatever the weather, there was riding. On Sundays the whole family went to church, bringing with them their pets, which were left in the churchyard during the service.

Sporting activities took up much of Lord Redesdale's time at Asthall. He did not hunt himself because of a back injury incurred as a young man, but he encouraged his children to do so, and always made sure they were well mounted. Shooting was his passion. He was an excellent shot, and had at Asthall one of the best shoots in that part of the country. He took the sport so seriously that on one occasion while out partridge shooting, Mark Ogilvie-Grant was sent home for laughing.

The older children were heartbroken to leave Asthall in 1926. Lord Redesdale's efforts to produce 'the best of everything for everybody' when planning and building Swinbrook were unappreciated by his family, who considered their new home hideous beyond belief, especially compared to the charming and attractive manor house they were leaving.

Near right Asthall Manor, near Burford, Oxfordshire
Far right, above The Hall at Asthall
Far right, below The Library at Asthall

During the six years at Asthall, the Mitford children were brought up in a similar way to those of most reasonably well-off land-owning families. They had, of course, some eccentricities, but what large family does not? The difference is that not every family has members with such literary talent and sharp powers of observation with which to describe their childhood.

The children were very much in awe of their parents. Lady Redesdale, despite her vague manner, was never unaware of what was going on, and could be very sharp if the occasion demanded. Lord Redesdale, when in a rage, was terrifying. Messiness with food infuriated him, which made meals in the dining room an ordeal for the younger children, though they were luckier than some in that they were never forced to eat what they did not want.

Lady Redesdale adhered strictly to the Mosaic food laws practised by her father. There was bacon and sausages for Lord Redesdale and the guests at breakfast, but this was never permitted for the children. When they dared, they would creep into the dining room, and smuggle out the forbidden fruit, though the joy of eating it was marred by the fear of being caught. Lady Redesdale's other foible was a complete mistrust of doctors and medicine. Prescribed pills and medicines were poured away, since, she claimed, the good body would cure itself. Inoculations were not allowed. 'Fancy pumping the good body with disgusting dead germs' was her view. Only appendicitis was taken seriously.

Lord Redesdale's favourites among his children varied according to his mood or their behaviour. Bringing a non-housetrained pet into the house meant an instant fall from grace, though his rages never lasted long, and the punishment was never more severe than being sent to bed. Only Tom, as the boy, could do no wrong.

The children went as far as they dared in teasing their father. Unity was the bravest. She had a technique of sitting at lunch and fixing her eye on him with, in Decca's words, 'a sombre, brooding glare'. This invariably infuriated him. But despite the rages, the children adored him. He was so funny, the instigator of many of the family jokes, and more 'human' than their detached mother.

The Mitford family at Asthall, 1922.
Back row: Nancy and Tom.
Middle row: Lady Redesdale, Diana, Pam, Lord Redesdale.
Front row: Unity, Jessica, Debo

Nancy on her hunter, Rachel

A page from Nancy's photograph album showing the Girl Guide camp at Eynsham, 1923

When Nancy was sixteen she had a short stay at a nearby finishing school at Hatherop Castle. Here, part of the course was Girl Guiding, which Nancy enjoyed so much that she persuaded her mother to let her start a company of Guides at Asthall. Lady Redesdale thought it was an excellent plan, and Diana and Pam were most unwillingly roped in to help. They were made to do this for a couple of years until Nancy's interest waned and the company was disbanded.

After Nancy had left Hatherop Castle her parents gave a dance for her at Asthall. This was before she had met any of the glamorous young men that were to become her friends, as is evident from her dance programme. Here her partners were either relations, such as Uncle Jack or Uncle Percy, or neighbours. David Hammersley was the son of Lady Redesdale's great friend Violet Hammersley, who used to stay with the family frequently. Nancy may have had this dance in mind when she wrote the following description in *The Pursuit of Love*.

This then is a ball. This is life, what we have been waiting for all these years, here we are, and here it is, a ball, actually going on now, actually in progress round us. How extraordinary it feels, such unreality, like a dream. But alas, so utterly different from what one had imagined and expected; it must be admitted, not a good dream. The men so small and ugly, the women so frowsty, their clothes so messy and their faces so red, the oil stoves so smelly and not really very warm, but above all, the men, either so old or so ugly. And when they ask one to dance (pushed to it, one cannot but suspect, by kind Davey who is trying to see that we have a good time at our first party), it is not at all like floating away into a delicious cloud, pressed by a manly arm to a manly bosom, but stumble, stumble, kick, kick.

The cooking range

G. G. Camp at Eynsham
July 27th – Aug 3rd
1923

Rita Nellie & the pig bucket

N.M. cooking

Nancy's programme for a dance at Asthall, 1921

Programme.	Engagements. N.M
1. VALSE "That Naughty Waltz"	David Flammessly
2. ONE STEP "Slippery Sam"	Mike
3. POLKA "See Me Dance"	Uncle Jack
4. FOX TROT "Indianola"	Cpt Cadogan
5. ONE STEP "Swanee"	Dick
6. FOX TROT "The Vamp"	Mike
7. ONE STEP "El Relicario"	Uncle Percy
8. FOX TROT "Dardanella"	Betty
9. VALSE "Sweet Hawaiian"	Teddy Moon
10. ONE STEP "Li'l Liza Jane"	Mr Fielden
11. FOX TROT "Peach Melba"	Alec Scott
12. ONE STEP "Sand Dunes"	John Dugdale
13. VALSE "Kissing Time"	Mike
14. COTILLON	Teddy Moon
15. GALLOP "John Peel."	David.

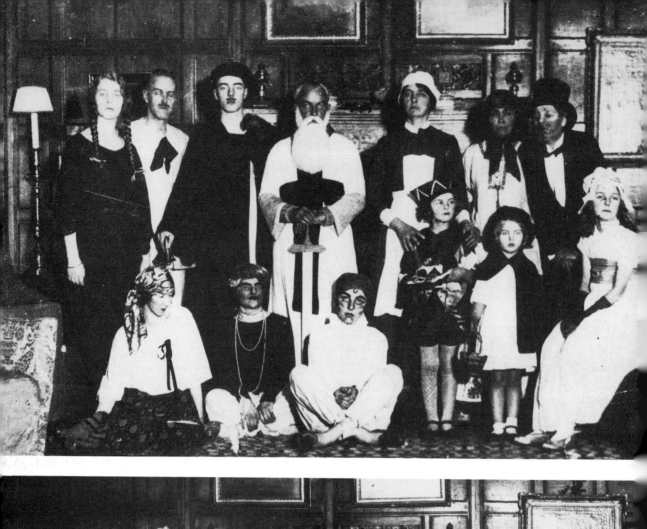

Pam's coming-out dance, 1925. Pam is standing, second from left,
Nancy fourth from left in a mantilla

Fancy dress parties and dressing up were Mitford
family passions, especially at Christmas. On
Christmas Eve the children all helped to decorate the
tree, and in the afternoon a party was held for the
children of the tenants and workers on the estate.
Lord Redesdale used to dress up as Father Christmas
and come in with a sack over his shoulder. All the
children were given a garment and an orange, quite
rare in those days and therefore considered a treat.

On Christmas Day the family went to chuch, where
Lord Redesdale read the lesson, but it was the evening
which was the most exciting part. Everybody would
rush up to the attic and get into fancy dress from the
dressing-up box. This was a great test of ingenuity as
the props and clothes were limited. Nancy was always
by far the best. One year she vanished without trace.
Everyone searched high and low, but it was some time
before she was discovered under the window seat
dressed up as a mummy.

But dressing up was not a passion for Pam, who
preferred to wear old sweaters and trousers and to be
outside looking after the animals. Therefore it is not
surprising she did not enjoy her coming-out dance
very much. 'I was supposed to be Madame de
Pompadour, but I felt very self-conscious because I
was rather fat. In fact, I did not enjoy any of the dances
that I went to when I came out, though I used to write
in my diary what a good time I had had. I suppose I
wrote it with an eye to be read in the future, and I did
not want to be considered a failure at parties.'

Left Christmas at Asthall in 1924 and 1925

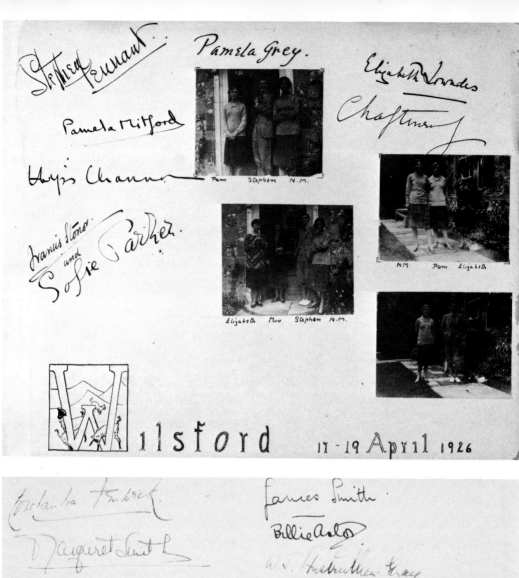

Stephen Tennant   Pamela Grey.   Elizabeth Lowndes

Pamela Mitford   Chastener

Thysis Channon

Francis Stone
and
Sofie Parker.

Pam   Stephen   N.M.

Elizabeth   Mou   Stephen   N.M.

NM   Pam   Elizabeth

Wilsford   11-19 April 1926

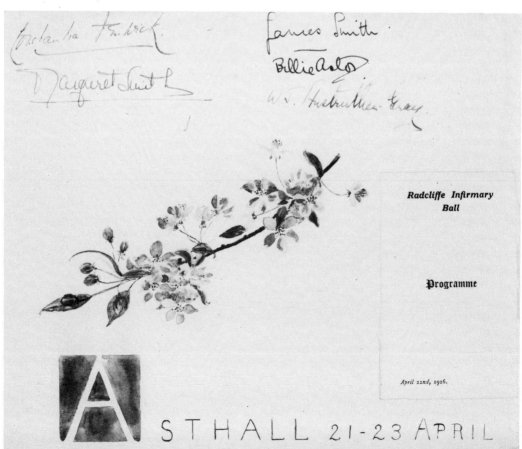

Constantia Fenwick   James Smith

Margaret Smith   Billie Aslop

                      W. Anstruther-Gray

Radcliffe Infirmary
Ball

Programme

April 22nd, 1926.

ASTHALL 21-23 APRIL

Dorothy Drury-Lowe
Johnny Drury-Lowe
Grizel Coube
Bobby Coube
Mark Ogilvie-Grant
Bryan Guinness
Nina Seafield
Jack Drury-Lowe

Mark, Nina & Johnny

Nina   Mark

Ballet! Mark & Nina

Johnny and friend

Mark

Nina

Locko 16-19 July 1926

A weekend at Locko Park in Derbyshire, the home of Johnny Drury-Lowe

Nancy lived at home until she was twenty-four, when she moved to London and shared a house with Evelyn Waugh and his first wife. When she was twenty, she had won a battle with her father to let her live in London and study art at the Slade. However, within a month she was home because her bedsitter had become so squalid. According to her, 'after about a week it was knee deep in underclothes. I literally had to wade through them. No one to put them away'. This was obviously worse than living at home, but all the same she found life at Asthall constricting, and welcomed visits away.

Nancy had made a lot of friends when she came out, a number of whom had been at Oxford, as she preferred the clever and the sophisticated. Mark Ogilvie-Grant was a great favourite of hers, though never a boyfriend in the accepted sense. Highly intelligent, he became a diplomat. Nancy used him as the model for the 'Wonderful old Songster of Kew' in

her novel *Pigeon Pie*. His sister, Nina, Countess of Seafield, was also a friend of Nancy's. Another clever friend was Stephen Tennant, son of Lord and Lady Glenconner and nephew of Margot Asquith. He was a poet, an artist, and one of the 'aesthetes', a set that included Harold Acton, Brian Howard and Cecil Beaton.

Nancy invited her friends to Asthall either for shooting weekends or for parties such as the Radcliffe Infirmary Ball, which was a yearly outing for the Mitfords. Generally these visits went off well, though the children were on tenterhooks lest any of the 'aesthetes' should provoke Lord Redesdale by not getting up in the morning, spilling their food, or making remarks that could in any way be construed as pro-socialist, pacifist or, worst of all, anti-empire. Mark Ogilvie-Grant was always popular because he liked blood sports and was able to get up. On one occasion he stumbled into the dining room at eight o'clock sharp to be greeted by Lord Redesdale with, 'Brains for breakfast, Mark!' This was all too much for the hungover guest, who hurried from the room.

Left above Staying at Wilsford, the Wiltshire home of the Glenconners

Left below A house party at Asthall for the Radcliffe Infirmary Ball

This photograph was taken during the Mitfords' last summer at Asthall before they moved to their newly-built house at Swinbrook. Posing for the yearly family photograph was considered by the children, especially as they grew older, as a great bore, and everyone ended up getting very cross. All the small pets had to be included in the photo, and it always took some time to get everyone arranged.

The animals played a very important part in the children's lives. They had ponies and were taught to ride from an early age, and they were encouraged to keep farm animals such as pigs, calves and chickens on a business-like basis. They had to pay a small rent to their father for a plot of land, but could keep whatever profits they made from the sales of eggs and the animals. Naturally they became fond of the creatures in their charge, and were agonized when they had to be sold to the butcher. Sometimes the children became so attached to them that they were turned into pets. Unity had a goat she adored, and Decca had a lamb called Miranda which she sometimes smuggled into her bedroom. The practice of keeping chickens made a deep impression on Nancy and Debo. In Paris, Nancy had a hen which wandered freely around the house, and, during the war, Debo managed to keep a few chickens in the back garden of her semi-detached house in Stanmore. Today, rare breeds of poultry strut around the garden at Chatsworth.

An old retired farmworker at Swinbrook remembers the children, each with a pet, coming to church in a donkey cart. The pets were left outside with the donkey, which brayed loudly at regular intervals during the service, invariably reducing the children to giggles.

When the Mitfords went to Paris in 1926, the only creatures they could take through quarantine were desert rats. These were concealed in their hotel rooms, much to the disapproval of Lady Redesdale who was terrified lest the chambermaids should find them and turn the family out of the hotel.

While they were living at Batsford, Lord Redesdale bought a shetland pony in London. The problem of getting it back to Oxfordshire was easily solved by taking the pony on the train, in the carriage with himself, Lady Redesdale, Nanny, the nursery maid and his four eldest children.

The Mitford family, 1926

Swinbrook House, Oxfordshire

After Batsford was sold in 1919, Lord Redesdale made plans to build a house on the site of an old farmhouse on the hillside above the village of Swinbrook. He set about this project with enthusiasm, intending to make an ideal dwelling for his family. However, Lady Redesdale, who understood better than her husband the finer points of comfort and interior decoration, refused to take any interest in the new house, and so as a result when it was finished, she and her older children were bitterly disappointed with their new home. One of its shortcomings was the bitter cold.

Central heating had been installed but never seemed to work properly, and the children were not allowed fires in their bedrooms. So, they used to sit in the linen cupboard, the only warm room in the house, which, known as the 'Hons Cupboard', was made famous by Nancy in her novels.

The family lived at Swinbrook from 1926 to 1935 when the house was sold, having been let on several occasions. Lord Redesdale decided to sell it when he realized that Tom was never going to be interested in running a country estate.

Tom at Eton, 1926

At the time of the move from Asthall to Swinbrook, Tom was at Eton where he was an Oppidan scholar (Oppidan scholars are boys who pass the scholarship into Eton but, unlike the King's scholars, they pay the full fees, and do not go into 'College', the special house for King's scholars). Unlike some of his sisters, Tom was a model schoolchild. Although he was good at all subjects, his outstanding talent was music, and in 1926 he won the school music prize for playing the piano.

The dining room at Rutland Gate

When Lord Redesdale sold Asthall in 1926, Lady Redesdale insisted that they should have a bigger London house. Pam and Nancy were grown up, spending more time in London, and the younger girls would need a proper base there when they were older. The house in Victoria Road was sold, and a much bigger one was bought in Rutland Gate in Knightsbridge. Lady Redesdale saved the French furniture from Asthall and, with her talent for decoration, she made the house pretty and original.

She was to regret spending all her time on the refurbishing of Rutland Gate, and not paying more attention to what Lord Redesdale was doing at Swinbrook, as she considered the careful creation of a house to be essential. The following description was found among her papers and diaries:

Three things come in order of importance. Husband, children, house. Of course, sometimes the order is altered and the children are first on the list – or even the house. It is the casket and setting for the whole, for the family, and if the woman of the house has no talent for painting or any of the arts, then it is her great opportunity to make something beautiful. The size or richness matters not at all. One small room can be lovely, and one hundred large rooms can be ugly, and often are. It has been my lot to live in many houses, and for this I am sorry, as I should have liked one house for the family, and the same one always to pass on to the next generation.

Lady Redesdale in her bedroom at 26 Rutland Gate, Knightsbridge, the London house of the Mitfords

Diana by Helleu, 1927

As a child, Lady Redesdale had met Helleu in Trouville while she was cruising with her father on his yacht. The artist remained a family friend, so that when Diana was in Paris learning French she spent much time with him and his wife. Helleu thought Diana beautiful and made several drawings and pen and ink sketches of her.

Diana loved her stay in Paris. Not only did she find the city beautiful and fascinating, but she also had much more freedom than she was accustomed to in England. In London young girls were not allowed to walk out, even to the shops, without a chaperon, and the Redesdales made no exception to this rule. In Paris, however, Diana had no trouble in making up excuses to give to her landladies, and had a wonderful time going to the cinema and out to dinner with young men.

Unfortunately this blissful life in France came to an abrupt end. Whilst in England for the Easter holidays,

Diana left her diary in the drawing room at Rutland Gate, where it was found and read by her mother. That Lady Redesdale might have been at fault in reading the diary seemed to occur to no one, and the outcome of Diana's carelessness was that she was not allowed to return to Paris: instead she had to return ignominiously to the schoolroom with her younger sisters.

However, life back in the schoolroom was for a short time only. The row, terrible as it had been at the time, was forgotten, and Diana had her first season in London in 1927.

By the time she was eighteen, Diana was a stunning beauty. Lady Lloyd considered her the most beautiful girl of her generation, and she had many admirers of all ages.

Right Diana, photographed by Lenare, 1928

The wedding of Diana to Bryan Guinness

Diana met Bryan, the eldest son of Colonel and Lady Evelyn Guinness, later Lord and Lady Moyne, in 1928, and was quick to recognize in him a kindred spirit. He was very good looking, sensitive and intelligent, and although he enjoyed aspects of country life such as horses and wild flowers, he was in no way one of the hearty sporting types so despised by the Mitfords. Diana considered him to be the epitome of the glamorous intelligentsia whose company she so desired. She was also fascinated by his parents, whose ideas on life and upbringing of children were so different to those of the Redesdales. Lady Evelyn never attempted to impose discipline on her children, and instead gratified their every wish. When her younger son Murtogh expressed a desire for a slide like one that he had played on at a fairground, Lady Evelyn had it built onto the staircase at their London home in Grosvenor Place, stretching from the top of the house down to the hall. She had a great passion for

Gothic, and decorated her houses accordingly, providing the guests with pewter plates and cutlery, and dressing the maids in sprigged cotton medieval gowns.

Bryan found Diana irresistible, and it was not long before he had proposed and been accepted. At first the Redesdales would not hear of the marriage, as they considered the couple much too young: they should wait for a year at least. However, supported by Bryan's parents, Bryan and Diana prevailed upon the Redesdales, who finally and reluctantly agreed. They were married in St Margaret's, Westminster, on 30 January 1929. Diana's beauty made her a popular model for artists. Apart from this portrait of her by Augustus John, she was painted by, among others, Henry Lamb, Adrian Daintrey, and the White Russian artist Pavel Tchelitchew.

Right Portrait of Diana by Augustus John, painted in 1931

Tom Mitford with Bryan and Diana at 10 Buckingham Street

After they were married, Bryan and Diana settled down in London at 10 Buckingham Street off the Strand, in a house designed by Edwin Lutyens. Diana loved the independence that marriage brought. Now she was able to entertain and to enjoy the intelligent and sophisticated company that she had so longed for. Henry Lamb, the artist, was a regular visitor, as were Henry Green, Roy Harrod and Lord Berners. During the first two years of her marriage Evelyn Waugh was her great friend and confidant. While she was expecting her son Jonathan, he would come and sit with her; he was to her the most perfect companion.

Waugh was one of the instigators of the Bruno Hat Exhibition. This was an amusing hoax in which Brian Howard executed some abstract pictures using cork bath mats and bits of rope. Tom Mitford played the part of the artist, sitting in a bath chair in eccentric clothes and talking in a strong German accent. Several well-known critics were invited and although the press found out it was a hoax, several people were completely taken in by the exhibition. Lytton Strachey bought a picture, though, according to Diana, this was more to please her than because of its artistic merit.

Henry Lamb, Darsie Jupp, Diana and Bryan in 1932

MR. BRUNO HAT came to England with his father in 1919 from Lübeck. After having lived in this country a short time, Mr. Max Hat married an Englishwoman, and bought a general dealer's shop in Clymping, Sussex, where he lived until he died in 1923. The shop is now managed by Mr. Bruno Hat with the help of his step-mother.

Mr. Bruno Hat is now thirty-one years of age. Apart from some two months or so at a Hamburg art school, he is entirely self taught. In frequent visits to London, exhibitions have provided him with little more than a glimpse of contemporary movements in painting. He has never, until now, exhibited a picture. A month ago, however, several examples of his work were taken to Paris, and the opinion there was so immediately favourable that successful arrangements have been made for an exhibition there in the early winter.

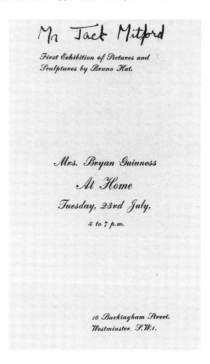

Mr Jack Mitford

First Exhibition of Pictures and Sculptures by Bruno Hat.

Mrs. Bryan Guinness
At Home
Tuesday, 23rd July,
4 to 7 p.m.

10 Buckingham Street,
Westminster, S.W.1.

Invitation to the Bruno Hat Exhibition, 1929

Nancy and Robert Byron at the Roman party

Diana as Empress Poppaea with John Sutr
at his Roman party in 1932

Fancy dress parties were all the rage in the 1920s and 30s; the more outrageous the better. In 1932 John Sutro, a film producer and contemporary of Bryan Guinness at Oxford, gave a Roman party, based on Cecil B. de Mille's recent film, *The Sign of the Cross*. Diana, representing Nero's Empress Poppaea, was, as always, surrounded by admirers. One of these was Peter Quennell, and his attentions provoked a furious reaction from his wife. In his autobiography, *The Marble Foot*, he described what happened:

Later that evening, a group of Roman Courtiers assembled round Poppaea's throne. S [his wife] was among us; but suddenly I saw her rise; and for the next few seconds I observed the whole scene in cinematic slow motion. Near the throne stood a magnum of champagne; or perhaps it was a jeroboam. Very gradually her sandalled foot lifted; slowly her right heel touched the bottle. It tilted; and a foaming flood of wine poured out over Poppaea's silken skirts. Whereupon S swiftly and quietly retired; and while the other courtiers offered their consolations and did their best to repair the irreparable damage, I angrily followed her out and called a taxi.

Diana remembers this incident well, though she says it was only a glass, not a whole bottle. She says also that Mrs Quennell had nothing to be jealous of as it was the most innocent friendship.

Cecil Beaton, Tilly Losch and John Sutro in 1934

Many of Diana and Nancy's friends, such as Cecil Beaton, Harold Acton and Brian Howard, were homosexual. Considering this was strictly illegal, these young men were daringly blatant, with their effete mannerisms and camp behaviour. Any suggestion of this would throw Lord Redesdale into a great rage, but Diana and Nancy considered it the height of sophistication and stylishness.

Biddesden House, near Andover, Hants

Bryan and Diana bought Biddesden House and its farm of two hundred acres shortly after they were married. It is an exceptionally attractive Queen Anne house built at the beginning of the eighteenth century for General Webb, one of the Duke of Marlborough's advisers. In the hall there is a large equestrian portrait of General Webb which, if removed, results in phantom hoof-beats up and down the stairs at night.

Diana decorated Biddesden with her characteristic style and good taste, and it soon became a centre for amusing and clever people. Henry Lamb was a regular visitor, as were the Sitwells, Cecil Beaton, and Lord Berners among others. Of all their friends Lytton Strachey and Dora Carrington, who lived nearby at Hungerford, were probably Diana's favourites, and

after their early deaths Biddesden was for Diana never quite the same again.

While Diana was in London giving birth to her second son Desmond, in September 1931, Bryan had the *trompe l'oeil* painted as a surprise for her return. It is a good example of Carrington's considerable talent as an artist, as well as a memorial to the artist so loved by Bryan and Diana.

In 1931 Pamela came to work at Biddesden as farm manager. She enjoyed the job and, considering the agricultural slump of those years, she made a fair success of it. One of her great joys was going to the Corn Exchange in Andover. All the corn merchants had their desks in the Exchange, and the farmers wishing to sell would take round samples, bargaining with the merchants. Pamela excelled at this and always got a good price for the Biddesden corn.

Right Trompe l'oeil in a window at Biddesden by Dora Carrington

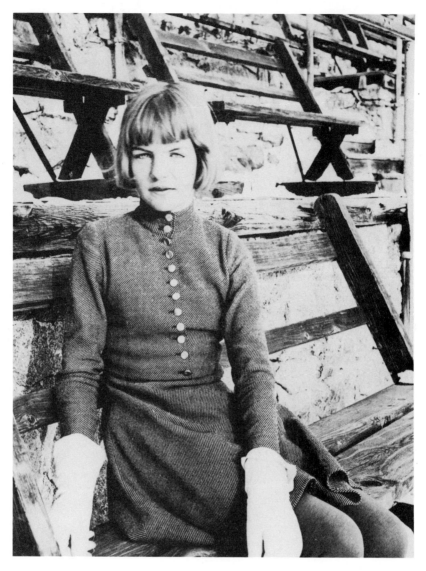

Debo at the ice rink, Suvretta House near St Moritz

At the age of eleven, Debo was such a talented skater that one of the selectors for the Junior British Team approached Lady Redesdale with a view to her being trained as a member of the team. Lady Redesdale refused to allow this as she realized that in order to be good enough to compete at international level Debo would have to devote her whole life to skating, and she felt her daughter should, at that age, have other interests as well. Debo was not told of this until many years later, and on hearing was understandably furious at the missed opportunity.

Debo on her pony with her mother and father at a meet of the Heythrop in 1934

Left and right Debo at Swinbrook in 1934

Opposite Lord Redesdale in Canada in 1934

Diana first met Sir Oswald Mosley at a dinner party in 1932, and thereafter they met frequently at parties that summer. Within a short time Diana had become spellbound by him, and after a few months she left Bryan Guinness to devote her life to Mosley and his cause.

Sir Oswald Mosley started his career in politics as Conservative MP for Harrow in 1918. In 1920 he left the Conservative Party because he did not agree with the coalition government led by Lloyd George in their policy towards Ireland, at the time fighting for its independence.

In the 1922 election Mosley defended and won again his seat at Harrow, this time standing as an Independent. However, he felt that he would not have the opportunity as an Independent member to put into action his plans for the country, so in 1924 he joined the Labour Party, winning his seat in a by-election in 1927 as MP for Smethwick. After the Labour victory in the 1929 general election the Prime Minister Ramsay MacDonald, impressed by his energy and ideas, gave him a job assisting J. H. Thomas in dealing with the problem of unemployment. After several frustrating and unsuccessful attempts to get Thomas to listen to his plans, Mosley gave up and went instead straight to the Prime Minister. But his ideas, produced in a document, *The Mosley Memorandum*, were rejected by the government, which was not confident enough to apply such radical solutions.

By 1930 Mosley had had enough of the Labour Party's vacillations and dilly dallying and resigned. Wasting no time, he launched his New Party, resulting in his expulsion from the Labour Party. The New Party was not a success, but as the Depression worsened, many people began to look for an alternative to the socialist government, and it was now that Mosley saw his chance, and so founded the British Union of Fascists.

Diana photographed by Cecil Beaton at a fancy dress party in 1932

Oswald Mosley in 1934. This photograph was on sale to supporters of the British Union of Fascists, and a postcard was made of it

The British, with their reputation for reserve and phlegm, feared fascism, because to many it represented revolution, violence and the destruction of democracy. News of events taking place in Germany confirmed these fears.

Despite this, Mosley's intelligence and obvious political ability ensured that he found supporters for his party. However, the rally at Olympia in 1934 represented the turning-point for the fortunes of the BUF, because from then on the media were solidly against Mosley and his party. Before this, newspapers of the Rothermere group, the *Daily Mail* and the *Evening News*, had supported him and given the forthcoming rally a lot of publicity. The communists, seeing a threat in the BUF, immediately organized their forces and infiltrated the rally, heckling and interrupting. Fights broke out, and a lot of people were hurt in the ensuing furore, but the press put the entire blame on the fascists. Lord Rothermere withdrew his support after Jewish advertisers threatened to boycott his papers, and from then on Mosley's meetings and his views were no longer reported.

Derek Jackson, incorrectly identified as Charles in the newspaper report, and Lord Berners were unlucky to get involved in the violence at Olympia with its attendant publicity, as they had gone out of curiosity and loyalty to Diana rather than from allegiance to the BUF.

After Olympia it became impossible for Mosley to speak at rallies uninterrupted, as the left wing always caused disruptions, often throwing dangerous missiles such as spearheads from railings. The BUF stewards normally managed to keep the agitators far enough away to prevent them from attacking the speaker, but they failed to do so at a rally in Liverpool in 1937, and Mosley received a nasty head wound from a brick that was hurled at close range. He was severely concussed and had to spend a week in hospital.

SATURDAY, JUNE 9, 1934.—Page 5

LORD BERNERS AND A "VERY RUDE P.-C."

Hit on Head at Olympia Disturbance

Lord Berners gave evidence at West London Police Court yesterday, when cases arising from the disturbances at the Fascists' rally at Olympia were dealt with.

Lord Berners was called by Charles Jackson (27), a physicist, of Cranleigh, Surrey. Jackson was fined £1 for obstructing the police.

Lord Berners said: "A policeman said to me very rudely, 'Get out' and hit me over the head with some sort of weapon like a sword. This naturally annoyed Mr. Jackson, who remonstrated with the officer, and I saw no more. He was carried off. I made a deposition on the matter at Kensington Police Station."

Lord Berners.

Jackson, replying to the magistrate, said that the police insulted him "in a most aggressive manner."

"You can't go about knocking people on the head as the police hit Lord Berners," said Jackson, "or hit people on the shoulder as they hit me. It is a most extraordinary thing to do."

Charles Jackson.

Sir Gervais: You must realise that the police had to deal with a disorderly or a potentially disorderly crowd.

Jackson: They were not disorderly. They were certainly singing their dismal little song, but the way the police acted was the most extraordinary performance I have ever seen. They did not even speak to me in the way I am accustomed to being spoken to. They did not call me "sir" or anything.

Report of Lord Berners and Derek Jackson appearing in court after disturbances at the BUF rally in 1934

Sir Oswald Mosley being attacked while
speaking at a BUF rally in Loverpool in 1937

In 1936 Diana decided to leave London and, since Mosley spent a lot of time campaigning in the north of England, it seemed practical to find a base in the Midlands. By great good fortune she discovered Wootton. The estate agent described it as a 'white elephant', but Diana immediately fell in love with the magical house. It was built in 1610 by Sir Richard Fleetwood, but as a Royalist stronghold during the Civil War it was attacked and besieged by Parliamentary troops. Left in a derelict, semi-ruinous state it was completely redecorated in 1700.

Left Wootton Lodge, near Uttoxeter, Staffordshire

Oswald Mosley, Kukuli von Arent and Diana at Wootton in 1936. Kukuli was the wife of Benno von Arent who designed the sets for many plays and operas in Germany during the 1930s

The Mosleys so dearly loved Wootton that before the war they spent all their holidays there rather than abroad. Apart from the house and its terraced garden, there was a park and a lake for riding and fishing, two of Sir Oswald's favourite occupations.

It was during their time at Wootton that Diana and Sir Oswald got married. The ceremony, which was kept secret until the birth of Alexander in 1938, took place on 6 October 1936 at Dr Goebbels' house in Berlin. Unity and Bill Allen were witnesses while Hitler, one of the guests, gave them a German eagle and a signed photograph as a wedding present. Apart from those who attended, only Lord and Lady Redesdale were told. The news came as a great relief to them, as they were very concerned at having a daughter who was not only divorced, but also living in sin.

Photograph of Nancy by Cecil Beaton

From Cecil.

Nancy was twenty and was still living at home when Beaton took this photograph. However, her intelligence and quick wit were beginning to be noticed. Brian Howard described her to Harold Acton as 'a delicious creature, quite pyrotechnical, my dear, and sometimes even profound, and would you believe it, she's hidden away among the cabbages of the Cotswolds'.

When Nancy was twenty-three she met and fell in love with Hamish St Clair Erskine, an eighteen-year-old homosexual who was then still at Eton. He was very fond of her, and flattered to be the object of her affections, but he was incapable of returning her love in the physical sense. Their affair, if it can be called that, ended early in 1933, and in November of that year, obviously on the rebound, she married Peter Rodd.

Rodd, or Prod, as he was nicknamed, was the son of Lord Rennell, the ambassador to Rome. He was clever, and superficially attractive, but despite Nancy's efforts to make their marriage work, living with him eventually became impossible, as he was a philanderer, often drunk, and usually jobless. He was not popular with Nancy's family. Debo described her brothers-in-law as 'The man Mosley, the Boy Romilly and the bore Rodd'. Because of Prod's inability to keep any sort of employment for more than a few weeks, Nancy had to work in order to try to earn some money to keep them both. But it must be said that had it not been for the need for money, Nancy's earlier books would probably not have been written.

The wedding of Nancy and Peter Rodd, 1933

When Nancy and Peter Rodd were first married they lived in Rose Cottage. The *Daily Telegraph* wrote an article, describing the house:

She has furnished and decorated in uncottage-like style the 300-year-old smugglers' cottage at Strand-on-the-Green. Beautiful pieces of Empire Furniture have been placed in the bow-windowed drawing-room, the walls have been painted lavender blue, and the curtains are Burgundy plush velvet hanging from pelmets that were formerly old rubbed gold picture frames.

Left Rose Cottage, Strand-on-the-Green, Chiswick
Below Nancy and Peter Rodd at Brighton in 1935

In the bedroom Nancy has reverted to the early Victorian style of ruffled curtains that let down from a pleated pelmet, like window blinds, instead of drawing from the side. These are made of pink cotton material to match the pink ceiling. A wallpaper that resembles quilting in grey upon cream provides the main decoration for this room. The sitting room hall has painted-style garlands on the cream walls, and the 300-year-old fireplace is still in use.

By 1935 Nancy had had three novels published, *Highland Fling, Christmas Pudding* and *Wigs on the Green.* They are all amusing in a light-hearted way, especially the first two, and they give a good picture of the attitudes and language of the younger generation in the 1920s and 30s. It was, however, her post-war novels that established her reputation as a novelist.

This was the last of the posed family photographs, taken in 1934. The older children were now grown up and going their separate ways. Nancy had married a few months earlier and was still sufficiently in love with Peter Rodd to tolerate his irresponsible ways. Diana, captivated entirely with Oswald Mosley, was in the process of divorcing Bryan Guinness. She was not very popular with her parents at this time, as they strongly disapproved of her leaving Bryan, and considered that she had led Unity astray by taking her to Nazi rallies in Germany the previous year. Unity had enjoyed herself so much, and had been so impressed that she returned to Munich by herself in 1934. She was twenty years old in this picture. On her shoulder she carries the pet white rat which she used to let loose at dances, throwing all the debs into complete panic.

Pamela was still managing the farm at Biddesden, but she gave that up later in the year and went on a tour of Europe. Decca was living at home, reading what she could about socialism and longing for escape from her rural existence. Tom was by now nearly qualified as a lawyer. Apart from his work at the bar he had many love affairs. One of his favourites at this time was Tilly Losch, the Austrian dancer who was married to the eccentric millionaire Edward James, and it was only James's affection for Diana that prevented him from naming Tom as the co-respondent in their very bitter divorce.

Debo, aged fourteen, was, apart from occasional bursts of adolescent discontent, happy with her life at Swinbrook. That her education was rather haphazard bothered her not at all, and unlike some of her sisters the thought of boarding school filled her with dread. The previous year she had been sent as a boarder to St Margaret's Bushey, but this was not a success. She had fainted in geometry because it was so incomprehensible, the hot blackberry and apple pie and custard had made her sick, and so, after three days of hell, her parents took her away.

The Mitford family at Swinbrook, 1934

Debo and Decca in 1935

In 1935 Debo's life in the country, centred round hunting and looking after her animals, satisfied her but Decca was asphyxiated by what she considered the boredom of country life. She did a season as a debutante, which she did not enjoy; she found all the young men very boring and narrow-minded, and none that she met seemed to share her left-wing sympathies. Nor could she find any kindred comrades in the Cotswolds.

Despite Decca and Unity's increasingly different views on politics, they were still great friends. At Swinbrook they had a private sitting room at the top of the house known as the DFD or 'drawing room from drawing room'. Here they could demonstrate their political differences. Decca describes it in *Hons and Rebels*:

At Swinbrook we lived in the DFD except for meal times. We divided it down the middle and Boud [Unity] decorated her side with Fascist insignia of all kinds – the Italian 'fasces', a bundle of sticks bound with rope: photographs of Mussolini framed in passe-partout; photographs of Mosley trying to look like Mussolini; the new German swastika, a record collection of Nazi and Italian youth songs. My side was fixed up with my Communist library, a small bust of Lenin

purchased for a shilling in a second-hand shop, a file of *Daily Workers*. Sometimes we would barricade with chairs and stage pitched battles, throwing books and records until Nanny came to tell us to stop the noise.

This was all done in good humour, but Decca realized their political differences were becoming serious enough one day to cause a rift. Her description of possibly losing a sister she loved because of political differences is sad and moving:

I still loved Boud for her huge glittering personality, for her rare brand of eccentricity, for a kind of loyalty to me which she preserved in spite of our now very real differences of outlook. When I thought about it, I had a sad and uneasy feeling that we were somehow being swept apart by a huge tidal wave over which we had no control; that from the distance a freezing shadow was approaching which would one day engulf us. Sometimes we even talked of what would happen in a revolutionary situation. We both agreed we'd simply have to be prepared to fight on opposite sides, and even tried to picture what it would be like if one day one of us had to give the order for the other's execution.

Right Decca dressed for presentation at court in 1935

Decca, Debo and Unity at Swinbrook in 1935

Photographs taken on the Hellenic cruise in 1936. Left to right: Adrian Stokes, Debo, Decca, Muv, Unity and Max Cholmondely

Muv with Unity, Jessica and Debo

In 1936 Lady Redesdale took Debo, Decca and Unity on a Hellenic cruise. Although Decca and Unity were by this time disagreeing about politics, the cruise was a success and enjoyed by them all.

Anita Leslie knew Unity well during the 1930s and gives an interesting and perceptive view:

She [Unity] was good-looking, but not a real beauty like Diana or Debo, and she hadn't got the literary brilliance of Nancy. But she was automatically close to me when we came out because we were both so *bored* by London Society. We needn't have been, for many of the young men we scorned would do brilliantly in the war, but they hadn't yet learned to polish themselves and we longed for an outlet – any outlet – so long as it was unconventional.

I can remember Unity telling me in thrilling undertones about the white slave trade, and how lovely it would be to get kidnapped, and wake up from the injection on a boat heading for South America. Apparently all one had to do was walk up and down Oxford Street, and sooner or later the prick of a needle would send one into oblivion. Unity used to do this regularly, but never got anaesthetized.

What we obviously needed was *work*, but jobs did not exist for debutantes then, save hatshops where one got paid two pounds a week to bring in one's friends.

In despair at the dullness of society life, I ran away on the stage and for a time I did not see Unity. When I came back to London she had met Hitler and was a dedicated Nazi. I saw a lot of her then, and in a way I could have easily fallen into her way of thinking if Hitler had not been so awful about the Jews.

I remember Unity dining with us the night that Diana bore her son to Oswald Mosley [Alexander in 1938] and how she kept leaving the table to telephone for news. Her face lit up when she talked about Hitler – by then she was well in with him – and I remember her very words describing Hitler's opinion of Anthony Eden – 'He says he looks like a clothes horse – so smart and his suits so well cut that there can be nothing in his brain.' Unity never spoke about her handsome S.S. officer [Erich Widemann] but she was obviously infatuated with the whole Nazi movement. As a debutante she had longed to be abducted by a brigand. Well, now she had found the greatest brigand in Europe – Hitler.

Unity in Crete during the cruise

Left to right: Diana, Josef Goebbels, Heinrich Hoffman and Albert Speer at Haus Wahnfried

Diana and Hitler at Haus Wahnfried

Left Tom and Diana, Munich, September 1936

Diana first visited Nazi Germany in 1933. She went out of curiosity after meeting in London Putzi Hanfstaengl who was then in charge of the Foreign Press Bureau. He told her that Hitler's Germany was not at all that the English papers made it out to be and that she should come over and see for herself. If she did so, he would arrange for her to meet Hitler. Diana agreed, and shortly afterwards she went, taking Unity with her for company. Putzi failed to introduce them to the Führer, but that did not prevent the sisters from being thoroughly impressed by what they saw.

Diana returned to Germany often after her first visit, and sometimes Tom would come over to see her. He spoke German fluently, having studied music in Vienna after he left Eton, and he had a deep affection for the country. He considered some of the aspects of the Nazi regime to be sound, particularly the way in which the country had been reorganized so efficiently, but he could never accept the anti-semitism as he had great respect for all the Jewish people that he knew in England.

While she was in Germany Diana sometimes used to stay at Haus Wahnfried, the family home of the Wagners in Bayreuth. Now it was owned and lived in by Winifred Wagner, the English-born wife of the composer's son, Siegfried. Hitler was a great admirer of Richard Wagner's music, and he first became friends with Siegfried and his wife in 1923. They supported him at the beginning of his rise to power, and when he was imprisoned after the unsuccessful Munich Putsch, Winifred sent him food parcels and the paper on which he wrote *Mein Kampf.* He was a frequent visitor to Haus Wahnfried, and it was one of his favourite places to go to relax from political pressures. Diana found Hitler fascinating company and, contrary to popular opinion, she says he did not hog the conversation, but liked discussions, especially about architecture and motor cars, about which he was very knowledgeable.

Other high-ranking members of the Third Reich used to go to Haus Wahnfried, some of whom are shown in the photographs. At this time Goebbels was Minister for Propaganda, Hoffman was Hitler's official photographer, and Albert Speer was Hitler's chief architect.

As the British Union of Fascists grew during the 1930s it became increasingly expensive to run and Mosley had to look for ways to raise funds. Bill Allen, an ex-MP in charge of the party's finances, knew of a fellow politician who was making a fortune through radio advertising by setting up a station in Normandy which was then beamed to England. The BBC did not approve, but it was popular with the public and so Mosley thought of setting up a similar station. He planned to try to get a concession from Germany, and as the country was very short of foreign currency he thought the idea might appeal. This took longer than expected; several years of negotiations and much travelling between Munich and Berlin, tasks usually given to Diana as she was able to speak German. Finally in 1938 she clinched the deal, but the following summer, when broadcasting was due to start, war was declared and the project came to nothing.

Diana preparing to go by air from Munich to Berlin

Diana with Bill Allen at a Nazi rally in 1935

Unity and Diana, with members of the SS marching in the background. This picture was taken by a photographer from the *Daily Mail* for a book by Ward Price, *I Knew These Dictators*. He wanted photographs of Diana and Unity, so they posed with a suitable background

It was at the Osteria Bavaria that Unity first met Hitler in February 1935. He often came to the restaurant for lunch, and once Unity had discovered this she became a regular customer in the hope of catching a glimpse of him. After seeing her there on several occasions, and noticing that she continuously stared at him, Hitler asked the manager to bring her over to his table.

So began a friendship that lasted until war broke out. He liked her because not only was she amusing and good company, but she was one of the few people with whom he could have a normal conversation. By 1935 Hitler was the unchallenged and unchallengeable ruler of Germany, powerful and feared. Most people were either trying to win favour with him in order to get themselves promoted to a position of authority, or otherwise were much too frightened of him ever to disagree. Unity was not interested in any power for herself, nor did she pose any threat, so Hitler felt free to discuss things with her without any fear of an ulterior motive on her part.

Stadelmann was one of Hitler's adjutants. Later he lost favour with the Führer and was put into a camp for a short time. Erich Widemann was Unity's steady boyfriend for several years. He worked in a photographic shop and was a part-time member of the SS.

Unity and Diana outside the Osteria Bavaria in Munich, 1935

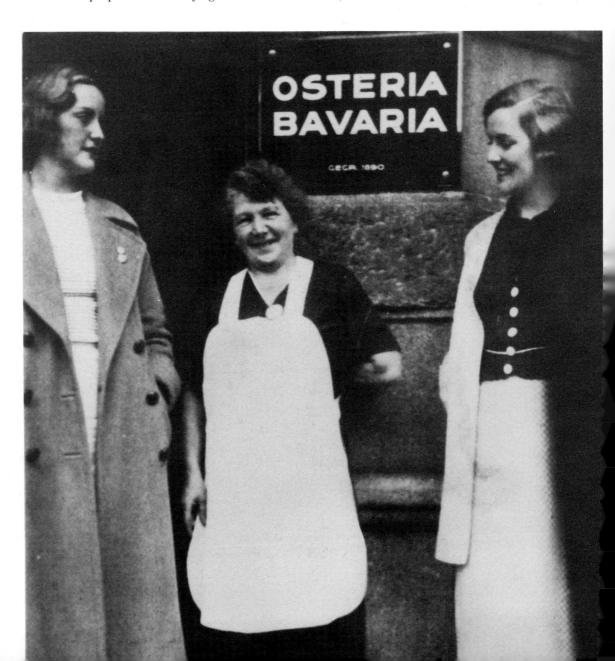

Left Unity and Herr Stadelmann outside the Brown House, Hitler's headquarters in Munich, August 1935

Below Herr Stadelmann, Unity and Erich Widemann on their way to the Berchesgarten, Hitler's house in the country

Bottom Hitler and his entourage arriving at the Osteria Bavaria

Unity at the Hesselberg Festival, 1935

In June 1935 Unity had written a letter to *Der Stürmer* proclaiming her anti-semitism. On receiving the letter, the editor, the infamous Julius Streicher, invited her to come to the Hesselberg Festival. This was supposed to be a folk music and dancing festival, but had become in effect a Nazi rally.

Unity accepted this invitation with alacrity. On the second day of the celebrations, Streicher, much to Unity's surprise, asked her onto the platform to speak. She was not expecting this, but she managed to make a short speech, saying that she hoped England and Germany would always be friends.

Photograph of Unity in the *Tatler*. The caption reads, 'A recent studio portrait of one of the ardent admirers of Germany's wonderful Führer, whom the Hon. Unity Mitford and some other members of her family know.'

Top right Unity at the Pension Doering with the Christmas tree given to her by Hitler in 1935

Above right Collage by Unity of Hannibal crossing the Alps

Opposite Unity and Hitler at Haus Wahnfried

From her first visit to Germany with Diana in 1933 Unity was fascinated and obsessed with Hitler and the Nazi movement. Indications of this are the lengths to which she was willing to go to catch a glimpse of the Führer. She was prepared for instance to sit up all night at Nuremberg station when there were no hotels available rather than miss the rally the next day, and she would lunch daily at the Osteria Bavaria on the chance that he might be there. When she finally met him in 1935, she wrote an eight-hundred-word letter to her father starting, 'Yesterday was the most wonderful and beautiful day of my life. I will try and describe it to you though I can as yet hardly write!' She went on to describe exactly what happened, and how incredibly lucky she was to have met Hitler, and that 'I am so happy I wouldn't mind a bit dying'.

What makes this obsession unusual is that it was never at any point based on physical attraction. She

was aware of, and accepted, Hitler's relationship with
Eva Braun. The fascination for the movement and its
leader grew more as a result of a need for a cause into
which to throw herself.

Accompanying this fascination was an
extraordinary naïveté. In 1934 there took place the
'Night of the Long Knives' in which Hitler arranged
the murder of Roehm and other leaders of the SA,
after being alerted to a plot to overthrow him. This was
a gruesome massacre in which a number of people not
involved in the plot were also murdered. Unity wrote
to Diana saying how sorry she felt for Hitler, especially
as Roehm had been such an old friend. The tone of the
letter was like that of one that might be written
describing somebody's grief at having a much-loved
pet pony put down, whereas the gruesome incident
Unity was describing had shocked all Europe.

On another occasion, Violet Hammersley, an old
family friend nearly sixty years old, went to visit Unity
in Germany. They attended a military parade, where
they were arrested by the Gestapo after Unity had tried
to take some photos. Stories of the Gestapo's brutality
were already legion in England, and Mrs Hammersley
was naturally terrified, but Unity treated the whole
incident as a huge joke. She wrote to Diana saying,
'wasn't it wonderfully funny that I should happen to be
arrested just when she was there'.

Unity made the collage of Hannibal crossing the
Alps as a birthday present for Hitler, and for
Christmas he sent her a decorated tree which caused
her enormous pleasure.

Decca in Portugal during the Hellenic cruise, 1936

Decca forged an invitation from the Pagets to stay in
Dieppe, knowing these friends were going to be in
Austria at the time, and therefore out of contact. The
Redesdales, suspecting nothing, agreed to this. Decca
and Esmond got away safely to France, and Decca
wrote to her mother in Dieppe to make her story
completely convincing. Esmond had trouble getting
Decca a visa for Spain, but finally achieved this by
getting one from the semi-independent Basque
Republic.

Meanwhile in London, the Redesdales began to
worry, as they planned a world cruise for which, by
now, Decca should have returned. Lady Redesdale
contacted an aunt of the Paget girls, only to be told
that the nieces had gone to Austria, not Dieppe, and
had not mentioned anything about taking Decca
Mitford. The Redesdales were frantic, and two days
passed before they were enlightened when one of
Esmond's friends arrived at Rutland Gate with an
explanatory letter from Decca.

Debo was hurt beyond measure that Decca, her
great friend and confidante, should have done such a
thing without telling her, though now she admits that
if she had known, she would have been in a terrible
dilemma as to whether she should tell her distraught
parents, or keep her secret.

The next step for the Redesdales was to try to get
them back. Peter Rodd suggested making Decca, who
was not yet of age, a ward of court, then anyone
attempting to marry her without the court's consent
could be sent to prison. This done, Nancy and Peter
were sent out to St Jean to try to persuade them to
return. The Rodds met the runaways, but could not
prevail on them to come back and, without an
extradition order, they were powerless to force them.

In March 1937 Lady Redesdale went to Bayonne,
where Decca and Esmond were living, and had a
friendly reconciliation with her daughter. It was
agreed that they could marry with the consent of both
sets of parents, and the wedding, attended by Lady
Redesdale and Mrs Romilly, took place in the British
Consulate in Bayonne on 18 May 1937.

Decca in her late teens had developed into a staunch
socialist, but found no opportunities in her sheltered,
chaperoned life to put her views to constructive use.
The Spanish Civil War, which broke out in 1936,
caused her even more frustration. She knew of people
from similar backgrounds to herself who had run away
to fight for the Republicans, and she longed to do
something for the cause. Opportunity came in January
1937. She went to stay with her cousin, Dorothy
Alhusen, and found to her joy her hero, Esmond
Romilly, who was recovering from dysentery
contracted while fighting in Spain.

It was love at first sight for them both, and between
them they arranged an elaborate plot to run away.

Right Decca and Esmond Romilly's wedding,
from Lady Redesdale's album

PERCY-RIMER, of Kenward, Aylmer, &c, to BARBARA, daughter of Mr. and Mrs. HUBERT HORSEY, of Midhurst, Fortis Green, N.2.
ROMILLY : MITFORD.—On May 18, 1937, at Bayonne, in France, E. ROMILLY to the Hon. JESSICA LUCY MITFORD.
TAUCHERT : WILCOX.—On May 15, 1937, at St. Andrew's Church, Ham Common, HANS EDWARD ... KAVANAGH, only daughter of Mr. ... Ham Common.

DIEU · ET · MON · DROIT

LONDON THURSDAY MAY 20 1937

JESSICA & ESMOND'S WEDDING

AT Hotel des Basques

18 May
1937

Mr Lopez

Mr _____

Mr O'hara

GUESTS

2007. - BAYONNE (B.-P.) - Rue Poissonnerie M. D.

The Romillys returned to England soon after their marriage, moving into a house in Rotherhithe which they shared with a friend of Esmond's, Roger Roughton. Esmond found a job as a copy writer in an advertising agency and Decca helped out occasionally by doing market research for the company. Her life in Rotherhithe was a complete contrast to that at Swinbrook, not least in that she now had to do the housework, a new experience which she found difficult and exhausting.

They had very little money, and Esmond's penchant for gambling tightened their budget further, but they were not short of amusements and used to give bottle parties for their friends. A regular guest was Esmond's

Left Decca in the late 1930s after her marriage to Esmond Romilly
Above Esmond Romilly, Decca and Philip Toynbee
Above right Decca and Esmond

old partner in crime, Philip Toynbee. They had become friends when, after running away from Wellington, Esmond produced a subversive magazine, *Out of Bounds*, which he arranged to have distributed around public schools by representatives in the hope of stimulating the pupils to rebel against the system. Philip Toynbee was the representative at Rugby and, inspired by the magazine, he, too, ran away. Together they joined forces with other communists to disrupt Mosley's BUF rally at Olympia in 1934 but, despite being well armed with knuckle dusters, Philip got badly beaten up.

In December 1937 Decca gave birth to a daughter, but their great happiness at this event was to be tragically short lived. Four months later the little girl caught pneumonia and died. Decca and Esmond were distraught. After spending three months in Corsica they returned to Rotherhithe, but the death of their baby made living there again too painful. Also, along with many other left-wing people, they were fearful of

Britain entering a pact with Germany. The prospect of this so appalled the Romillys that they began making plans to emigrate to America.

Rignell House, near Banbury, Oxfordshire

In December 1936, Pam married Derek Jackson, the son of Sir Charles Jackson, one of the founders of the *News of the World*. Derek was a physicist of exceptional brilliance. After getting a First at Cambridge, he went to work with Professor Lindemann at the Clarendon Laboratory at Oxford. By the age of twenty-two his name was known in scientific circles throughout the world for his discoveries and work in the field of spectroscopy. At a relatively young age he became a Fellow of the Royal Society, and later, when he worked in France, an Officer of the Legion of Honour.

His marriage to Pam was his second; he had previously been married to Poppet John, the daughter of the artist Augustus. He was to marry a further four times after his divorce from Pam in 1950. Pam's wedding outfit was black, a colour considered by many as unlucky for a bride. For Pam and Derek there was to be something in this superstition. The next day, Derek's adored twin brother Vivian was killed as a result of being flung out of a sleigh and hitting his head on a milestone. Those who knew Derek before Vivian was killed say he was never the same again.

Derek was very eccentric, and as is generally the case with such people, cared not a jot for what others thought. Some of his behaviour caused Pam great embarrassment, especially his penchant for pulling the communication cord on trains. He did this on one occasion, and when the guard, expecting some catastrophe, rushed up to find out what had happened, Derek said, 'I'll tell you what has happened. Your communication cord is filthy. Look what it's done to my glove.' He also loved to shock. To some staid acquaintances he said, 'They sent me to Berlin when I was young to teach me to like women. So I picked up a blonde on the street, and when we got upstairs, thank God, it was a boy.'

After they were married, Derek and Pam lived at Rignell, Derek's house which he had bought some years before as it was near Oxford, and well placed for hunting with the Heythrop. He continued to work at the Clarendon until war broke out, when he joined the RAF. He fought with great bravery, winning the DFC in 1941. Later when he was working on the development of 'window', strips of metal paper which affected enemy radar, he was awarded the AFC for his courage in testing a captured enemy aircraft.

Those in charge of the Air Ministry and Air Force made excellent targets for Derek's teasing. When flying he used to shout instructions to his pilot in German, and on one occasion, having been sent for by Whitehall to give a report on his research into German radar, he merely said, 'The machine was so pretty I wanted to stroke it', adding that there was no point explaining his discoveries as none of those present would understand.

Right The wedding of Derek Jackson and Pam at Caxton Hall 29 December 1936. Lord and Lady Redesdale are on either side of Derek and Pam. Diana and Nancy are on the left in the next row with Tom on the far right

Apart from science, Derek's great love was horses. As an amateur rider he gained many successes under National Hunt rules and twice finished in the Grand National on his steeplechasers, Tulyra and Princess Mir. Derek loved to provoke the Jockey Club stewards, something very few of those in racing dared do, since they held absolute power and had the authority to impose fines, suspensions and withdrawal of licences. Derek was frequently being fined for various misdemeanours, and on such occasions he would give the stewards a £100 note and ask for the change. On one occasion, having been fined £10, he gave them £12 saying, 'There you are, £3 each.'

Hunting he loved, and during the season he would go out two or three times a week. His enthusiasm was such that one day, having jumped into a pond and got soaked, he rushed home, changed and returned to the hunt.

In 1947 Derek and Pam decided to live in Ireland. The high rate of taxation imposed by the Labour Government meant that Derek would have to start economising by cutting back on his racehorses and scientific research. This, plus the fact that he could not tolerate the prospect of being ordered around by socialists, provoked him into leaving England. Ireland seemed a good choice, as it is a perfect country for anyone who loves horses. Pam and Derek rented Lismore from Debo and Andrew and set about finding a house. This took some time, as so many of the promising sounding houses turned out to be roofless ruins. Eventually, however, Ikey Bell, the famous huntsman, found them Tullamaine.

Pam loved living in Ireland. She used to ride every day and helped to manage the farm, and there were plenty of interesting and amusing people living nearby so she was not short of company. Derek loved it too, but eventually he found there was not enough to satisfy his brilliant brain and in 1950 he left Ireland. Pam remained and continued to run the farm, but by the late 1950s it had become such an uphill struggle that she sold the house and land and came back to England to live in the Cotswolds.

Pam and Derek Jackson at a meet of the Heythrop Hounds in 1938

Pam with Mrs Dudley Delavine

Derek on Sedia Gestatoria at Windsor Races, spring 1939

Below Tullamaine Castle, Co. Tipperary

William Acton was the brother of Diana and Nancy's great friend Harold, one of the original 'aesthetes' at Oxford in the 1920s. William drew a pen and ink portrait of Diana in 1937, and Lady Redesdale liked it so much that she commissioned him to do drawings of all her daughters. She did so just in time, as 1938 was the last year in which all the sisters were in England and available for sittings.

Lady Redesdale and Debo at the Grand National in 1937

Debo was a debutante in 1938, a vintage year for beauties. According to a contemporary, Lady Lloyd, Debo was 'very amusing, and very beautiful and therefore very popular. She almost always wore tulle dresses with large crinolines, which made her stand out as that was an unusual style for the 1930s.'

Unlike Decca, Debo loved her time as a debutante. It was a very different life for girls before the war. During 'the season' Debo went to a dance every night, with Lady Redesdale always attending as chaperon. Looking back, Debo realizes what an effort this must have been for her mother as she was not really sociable

and hated staying up late. However, she dutifully did it for all her six daughters. She was a strict chaperon, and once took Debo home early for dancing three times in succession with the same man, which then was considered very bad form.

Debo met her future husband, Lord Andrew Cavendish, the younger son of the 10th Duke of Devonshire, when they were both eighteen, shortly after he had left Eton. For her, there was never really anyone else, and for the next two years they were secretly engaged before being considered old enough to announce it officially.

The 1930s had been a period of considerable change and upheaval for the Redesdales. Shortage of money had forced Lord Redesdale to sell his Swinbrook estate, and now they divided their time between Rutland Gate, the Old Mill Cottage at Swinbrook and Inch Kenneth, an island off Mull bought in 1938. Apart from their financial worries, their children had caused them great concern.

When Diana left Bryan Guinness, the Redesdales were appalled. Divorce was the ultimate diagrace to the family. Debo was forbidden to see Diana and Mosley, even after the secret marriage was revealed. Decca's elopement had worried and upset them, but these dramas were relatively minor compared with the consequences of Unity's adherence to Fascism. In the early thirties, news of Nazi atrocities began to circulate in England, so that when the Redesdales discovered Diana had taken Unity, aged nineteen, to a Parteitag, they were horrified.

In 1934, Unity persuaded her mother to visit her in Munich. Sydney enjoyed her visit but could not share Unity's wild passion or become an immediate convert to the cause. The following year Lord Redesdale paid a visit. Despite the fact that he had loathed the Germans on principle since the First World War, Unity found him a far more satisfactory guest, getting on 'wonderfully with the sturmführers'. Three years later both parents visited Unity again and were taken to lunch with Hitler. Unity write to Diana, 'Farve really does adore him in the same way as we do, and treasures every word and every expression'. This is probably an exaggeration by Unity, but the fact that this took place as late as 1938, when Britain's relations with Germany were strained, is significant. However, by the time war broke out, Lord Redesdale had reverted to his original opinions of the Germans and joined the rest of the nation in wholeheartedly condemning them. Sydney refused to agree: she had been impressed with what she had seen on her visits to Unity and stuck to these views for the rest of her life. So acute was their disagreement, that in the end the Redesdales were forced to live apart.

Lord and Lady Redesdale in 1939

now in Brixton Prison, Diana returned to Denham where her telephone was tapped and the house placed under surveillance. A month later she, too, was arrested. The policewoman told her to bring enough clothes for a couple of days, so Diana, expecting to return after the weekend, left her six-week-old baby, Max, at home. However, her expectations of a short visit were proved quite wrong. She and her husband remained in gaol without a trial for three and a half years, only to be released when Sir Oswald became dangerously ill. They were released not on compassionate grounds, but for fear that if he died he would become a martyr.

For the first year and a half Diana was in Holloway and Mosley in Brixton, but Tom Mitford persuaded Winston Churchill to let them be together. As a result

Nanny Blor with Alexander, aged two, and Max, aged fourteen months, at Rignell in 1941

Lady Redesdale's permit for visiting Diana in Holloway

The outbreak of the Second World War brought tragedy in full measure to the Mitfords. For Unity it meant life was no longer worth living, for the Redesdales the breaking up of their marriage after nearly forty years, and for Diana and Mosley, many years in prison.

Sir Oswald was arrested on 24 May 1940. A policeman arrived quite suddenly at their flat in Dolphin Square with a warrant, and marched him off. That Mosley had done nothing illegal made no difference. He was arrested under Defence Regulation 18b, a convenient law which allowed the government to arrest anyone arbitrarily whom they considered had been or had potential to be a danger to democracy. Not only could people be arrested under this regulation, they could also be imprisoned indefinitely without trial.

Having, with difficulty, secured a lawyer for Mosley,

they were moved to a house in the prison grounds called the Private Detention Block. Naturally, any sort of material comfort was non-existent, but their pleasure at being reunited made the appalling conditions of prison much more bearable. They looked forward enormously to the weekly visits of their families, who would bring what they could in the way of food, sometimes smuggling in port or brandy.

Diana missed her baby sons, Alexander and Max, enormously, but at least she knew they were safe and being well looked after. After her retirement, Nanny Blor frequently went to stay with her old charges in their various homes, and was as much loved by the next generation of Mitfords as she was by their mothers.

Diana and Alexander with Sir Oswald Mosley shortly before his arrest in 1940

Debo wearing her white organdie wedding dress made by Victor Stiebel

Debo and Andrew Cavendish's wedding took place the day after a particularly devastating air raid. A house in Rutland Gate was completely destroyed and, two hundred yards away, the Redesdales' house had all its windows blown in. It was too late to change the plans for the reception to be held there, but Lady Redesdale solved the problem with great ingenuity by hanging up strips of wallpaper to simulate the curtains that had been destroyed in the blast.

Among the telegrams received was one from Kathleen Kennedy, engaged to Andrew's brother, the Marquis of Hartington, and her brothers Joe and Jack. Another came from the Mosleys, in prison. Diana had made friends with one of the wardresses, who agreed to send the cable for her.

FONDEST LOVE DARLING AND BEST WISHES FOR YOUR HAPPINESS FROM DIANA AND KIT

HAVE JUST HEARD GOOD NEWS COULDNT BE MORE PLEASED CONGRATULATIONS MUCH LOVE TO YOU BOTH

JOE JACK KICK KENNEDY

Left Debo on her wedding day, 9 April 1941, at St Bartholomew-the-Great, Smithfield, being given away by Lord Redesdale

Debo registering for National Service, April 1941

After Debo was married she had to go straight from her wedding reception, in her going-away clothes, to register for National Service. She and Andrew went on honeymoon to Compton Place, a house belonging to Andrew's parents at Eastbourne. It was the time of the heavy air raids, and every night they heard the German bombers on their way to London and then returning again some hours later.

Debo was never called up for National Service because she became pregnant and subsequently had three babies in the first four years of her marriage,

Debo and Andrew's wartime home in Brockley Avenue, Stanmore

though she did work in a YMCA canteen, where all the other workers teased her about her accent.

Part of the war was spent living in Stanmore, Middlesex, as Andrew was stationed nearby. By a pleasant coincidence Derek and Pam had a house in the same road, as Derek's fighter command was at Stanmore. The war years were very different from the carefree times Andrew and Debo and their friends had enjoyed in the late 1930s. Like everyone else, they had many friends killed fighting, and both of them lost their only brothers. Debo had the added sadness of witnessing her parents' marriage, once so happy, disintegrating as a result of their political disagreements. She had always remained on excellent terms with both of them and, as she loved them dearly, the splitting up was, for her, all the more painful.

On top of this, Unity's Fascist sympathies, and Mosley and Diana's political organization had resulted in a lot of bad publicity. When war broke out the press whipped up an almost hysterical hate campaign against them which lasted throughout the war. As a result of this, all members of the family, whatever their political views, sometimes had to have police protection.

Right Debo with police escort

Unity at Swinbrook in 1943

Unity with Lord and Lady Redesdale at the Old Mill Cottage, Swinbrook, in 1942

Apart from occasional visits home, Unity remained in Germany until war was declared. What she had dreaded most in the world had finally happened; that the two countries containing all those whom she loved most should be at war was too much for her to bear, and on 5 September 1939 she shot herself in the Englischer Garten in Munich.

She failed in her attempt to kill herself, but the bullet went through her forehead to the base of her skull, and she was dangerously ill. Hitler kept in close touch with the hospital, and when she was considered well enough he arranged for her to be taken to Switzerland in an ambulance train, where she was met by her mother and Debo.

Unity spent a lot of the war years with her parents at the Old Mill Cottage. The cottage had been sold along with the manor house and the village in 1935, but the Redesdales rented it back just prior to the war.

Unity never recovered from her attempted suicide. The bullet, which was lodged in her skull, damaged her brain irreparably, leaving her like a child. However, she was able to drive and she attended parties. Charles Ritchie, the diplomat and diarist, met her at a party of Nancy's and 'liked her better than anyone else [there]. She has something hoydenish and rustic about her'.

Lady Redesdale devoted herself to looking after Unity, which was not always an easy task as the brain damage caused her to have frequent outbursts of rage and irrational behaviour. Apart from this, it caused the Redesdales great pain to see their once cheerful and lively daughter reduced to a remnant of her former self. Lord Redesdale, who had a phobia about messiness and things being spilt, could not bear to be with her for long periods. He moved to Inch Kenneth, while Sydney and Unity lived either at Swinbrook Cottage or at Old Mill Cottage, High Wycombe. At the end of the war, Sydney and Unity moved up to Inch Kenneth, and David went to live at Redesdale, a village in Northumberland where his mother had spent her last years.

Unity lived for nine years with the bullet lodged in her brain, but in May 1948 a bout of meningitis caused the bullet to move, which proved fatal. She was buried in the churchyard at Swinbrook, under a headstone bearing the epitaph, 'Say Not the Struggle Naught Availeth'.

Tom Mitford in 1944

This was one of the last photographs to be taken of Tom. He was thirty-six when he was killed. Up to 1939 he had been practising as a barrister, but when war broke out and he joined up, he found he enjoyed army life so much that he had intended to continue as a regular soldier when the war was over.

He spent two years fighting in North Africa, and was then posted to Burma. This was at his request, as he did not want to fight in Germany directly against the people of a country he had loved.

In early April 1945 he was shot in the stomach by a sniper and died of his wounds a day later.

In February, 1939 Decca and Esmond Romilly emigrated to America. They had been given plenty of contacts by their left-wing friends in London, and so they quickly got to know people. After trying various jobs, Esmond ended up working in a bar in Miami, which he proved to be extremely good at, as the bar went from strength to strength.

Decca and Constancia

When war broke out in September the Romillys remained in America and in 1940 Esmond volunteered for the Canadian air force. This, he made clear, was not out of patriotism for England, but from a heartfelt obligation to fight Fascism. He trained as a navigator and was sent to Britain in the summer of 1941. In November, during the heavy bombing raids on Germany, he was among those who failed to return from a mission to Hamburg.

Constancia was born in summer 1940, and was the one comfort for the shattered Decca. After the death of Esmond, Decca showed her true fighting spirit. Instead of returning to her family in England for moral and financial support, she stayed true to her ideals. She learnt to type, getting a job as a typist for the Office of Price Administration. She was soon promoted and her life, despite her tragic and irreplaceable loss, began to take a turn for the better. Through her work she met Bob Treuhaft, a brilliant lawyer with Communist sympathies who did laudable work in defending those who could not afford to pay legal costs. Within a few months they were married.

Crowood House, Ramsbury, Wiltshire

After their traumas and experiences during the war, the Mosleys were able to settle down to a comparatively normal existence at Crowood, where they lived from 1945 until 1951. Sir Oswald ran the farm, rode and shot as he had at Wootton before the war. Some of the local gentry attempted to show their disapproval by ignoring their new neighbours, but this, insofar as she noticed, came as a relief to Diana. Like her father, she had never been keen on 'county' life. Anyway, they were not short of friends nearby;

John and Penelope Betjeman lived at Wantage and Lord Berners was a regular visitor from Farringdon.

When the war ended, Regulation 18b was lifted, and the Mosleys were free to travel round England unguarded. But rumours to the contrary apparently abounded, as one day Diana answered the door bell to find two young RAF officers who had come up to the house for a bet, having heard that it was so closely guarded as to be impenetrable.

Right Diana and Oswald Mosley
with their two sons, Max and Alexander

After the war Oswald Mosley restarted his party, which he now called the Union Movement. However, the war and the Nazi atrocities, which were now being revealed in their full horror at the Nuremberg trials, had given the word Fascism a terrifying new meaning. The people of Britain looked forward to peace and the happier days ahead promised by Attlee's Labour Government, and Mosley found it hard to regain the support that he had had in the 1930s.

In 1950, therefore, the Mosleys were making plans to leave England, as the bias of the authorities towards them showed no sign of abating. Crowood was sold, and Diana and Sir Oswald bought one house in Ireland and another near Paris. The two houses could not have been more different. The Irish house, at Clonfert, East Galway, was an old bishop's palace, with an ancient yew avenue surrounded by the bog that covers so much of that part of the country. Max, now aged eleven, was in his element, adoring the marvellous hunting for which Ireland is so famous.

The house in France, the Temple de la Gloire in Orsay, is a beautiful Directoire pavilion, built in 1800. It is small, but grand and elegant, and Diana and Sir Oswald fell in love with it at first sight. It is now the permanent home of Diana.

Alas, Clonfert burnt down in 1953. Faulty wiring, the bane of Irish houses, caused the blaze, which engulfed the house before help arrived, destroying all the Mosleys' furniture, pictures and belongings.

Diana at a Union Movement rally in 1948

Right Diana in 1950

The Mosleys' yacht, *The Alianora*

Diana at the Lido in Venice, 1954

After the war and their imprisonment, the Mosleys were greatly looking forward to going abroad and having their first proper holiday for years. But the Labour Government, without giving any reason, refused to provide them with passports. For two years they applied, each time being refused. Then Mosley discovered in, of all places, the Magna Carta that there was nothing to stop anyone leaving England. This stipulation had never been changed, and passports were only required by law to *enter* a country. So, Mosley got in touch with General Franco, who said they would be welcome to land in Spain with or without a passport. Sir Oswald bought a 60-ton yacht, *The Alianora*, and the family began to make arrangements to leave. The Government then realized that they were going to be made to look fools, and granted the passports shortly before the Mosleys departed.

The Alianora was sold in 1950, and from then on the Mosleys spent every summer holiday in Venice. Here they found many friends, such as Daisy Fellowes, the Singer sewing machine heiress who was a close friend of Nancy in Paris, and Charles de Beistegui, owner of the fabulous Palazzo Labia.

Apart from the parties and friends, and the pleasure of hot days spent swimming at the Lido, the Mosleys loved the beauty of Venice. Sir Oswald said of it, 'If beings from another planet came to earth, they would imagine Gods must have built this city.'

As well as their holidays in Venice there were frequent visits to Debo in England, and the purchase of Clonfert in Ireland in 1951 enabled them to see plenty of Pam in nearby Tipperary. The Mitfords' cousin Robin Rodzianko also lived in Ireland, where her husband Paul, a White Russian who had escaped during the Russian Revolution, was training the Irish equestrian team.

After they moved into the Temple de la Gloire, the Mosleys quickly acquired a big circle of friends in Paris, including the Duke and Duchess of Windsor. The Duke and Mosley were both exiles from a country they had loved, and which they had been prepared to serve, so that they felt a strong sympathy with each other. The Mosleys enjoyed their parties at the house in the Bois de Boulogne or the Moulin de la Tuilerie not far from Orsay, for the Duchess was an excellent hostess who always had delicious food and good company. After the Duke's death, the lonely and ailing Duchess relied on Diana as a companion and confidante.

The Temple de la Gloire, Orsay

Above Paul Rodzianko, Diana, Sir Oswald Mosley and Diana's Aunt Daphne at Tullamaine in 1951

Below The Duchess of Windsor and Sir Oswald Mosley at her house in the Bois de Boulogne

The wedding of Billy Hartington to Kathleen Kennedy.
Left to right: the Duchess of Devonshire, Billy and Kick, Joe Kennedy,
the 10th Duke of Devonshire

Billy Hartington was Debo's brother-in-law, her husband Andrew's elder brother. Kathleen Kennedy, or Kick as she was always known, was the daughter of Rose and Joe Kennedy. Although not a beauty, she had immense charm and was loved by everyone who knew her. Billy and Kick were married in May 1944, and she and her husband had only five weeks together before he left with his regiment for France. He was killed by a sniper in Belgium on 9 September.

After she was widowed, Kick divided her time between her own family in America and living in London in a house in Smith Square, Westminster. She was killed in an aeroplane accident in 1948, and was buried in the churchyard at Edensor, the village in the park at Chatsworth. After she was widowed she remained a great friend of Debo's, had hosts of admirers and was welcome everywhere. To the English, her Boston accent was very amusing, as was her continued surprise at the English way of life. Part of her great charm was that she was very easily pleased, and had the knack of getting on with everyone, whatever their walk of life or background might be.

The one thing that the Devonshires had dreaded was that their children might marry Catholics. But when the 10th Duke and his Duchess met Kick they loved her, and their very strong prejudice was forgotten.

eft Debo and Kick in 1944

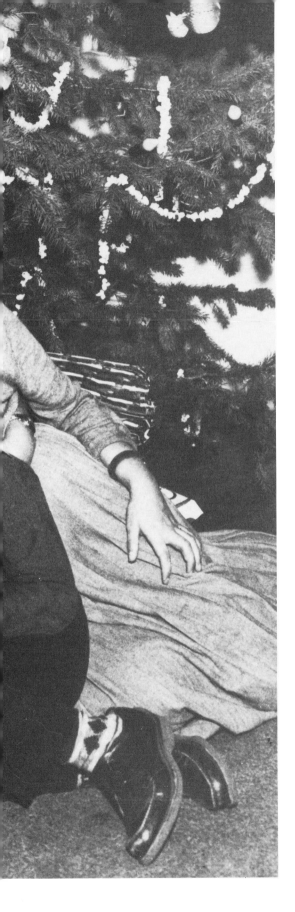

The Treuhafts moved to Oakland, California, in 1947, where they continued to work hard for the Communist Party in America. They left the party in 1956, but continued to support and campaign for left-wing causes.

It was during the 1950s that Decca began her writing career. Her first venture into print was a pamphlet called 'Lifemanship, or How to Become a Precisely Because Man'. In some ways it resembled Nancy's *Noblesse Oblige*, but rather than delineating the difference between upper- and middle-class choice of words, Decca showed how Marxists misused the English language, i.e., using pleonasms like 'life itself' rather than just 'life'. Cheered by its success, Decca wrote *Hons and Rebels* about her life up to Esmond's departure to fight. Although her sisters and others consider the book strays from the truth, and it was in some respects hurtful to her family, it is no doubt a very funny book as well as a moving one. When it was published, it was an immediate success both in England and America (where it was published under the title *Daughters and Rebels*).

Her next project was a very amusing exposure of the American funeral parlour business, already parodied in Evelyn Waugh's novel, *The Loved One*. Decca's book, *The American Way of Death*, revealed in its author a genius for investigative writing, and it remained on the bestseller list for weeks. She put this talent to further use in several more books, including *Kind and Usual Punishment*, an exposure of the treatment of prisoners in American gaols, and *The Making of a Muckraker*, a collection of journalism.

Decca with her husband Bob Treuhaft, their two sons, Benjy and Nicholas, and Decca's daughter Constancia Romilly, in the early 1950s

The war changed Debo and Andrew's future completely. As the younger son, Andrew had expected to have to find a job and get on with earning his living as soon as the war ended. But, in 1944, his elder brother, Billy Hartington, was killed leaving Andrew heir to the title and estates, which he inherited in 1950 on the death of his father. However, apart from the huge responsibilities and hard work that go with running large estates, Debo and Andrew welcomed the chance to travel and enjoy themselves, which came as a great joy after the austerity and restrictions of war-time.

Venice was one of their favourite places for holidays, and it was here that Debo and Andrew attended the famous Beistegui Ball in 1951. This was held in the Palazzo Labia, the newly restored house of Charles de Beistegui, and was without doubt the fancy dress ball of this century. The guests had to be dressed in eighteenth-century clothes, and Debo wore a dress of pale blue silk trimmed with white muslin which was copied from a miniature of Georgiana, Duchess of Devonshire. Although pretty, her costume was, she says, lost amongst the other incredibly imaginative and glamorous creations that were to be seen that evening.

After the war, the South of France quickly regained its pre-war popularity. Debo frequently went there to stay with Prince Aly Khan at his villa, Château L'Horizon. She always loved her holidays there, as the hot weather, delicious food and company of film stars offered a complete contrast to English country life.

Like her sisters, Debo adored Evelyn Waugh and, except when he was drunk, found him the perfect companion. He gave her a hat which he had bought in Paris, as he said now that she was a Duchess she should have something suitable in which to open fêtes.

Debo dressed for the Beistegui Ball in 1951

Debo in a hat given to her by Evelyn Waugh

Prince Amin Aga Khan, Lady Anne Tree, Peregrine Hartington,
Prince Aly Khan and Debo at Lismore in 1951

Debo at Château L'Horizon, 1954

Violet Hammersley, a life-long friend of Lady Redesdale, was beloved by all the Mitfords. In 1903, aged twenty-four, she had married a widower of nearly fifty. He died ten years later leaving her a rich widow with three children. However, the bank of which he had been a partner, and which contained all her money, collapsed in 1923, leaving her comparatively poor, a fact that she continued to bemoan for the rest of her life. She remained a friend of all the children as they grew up, and frequently visited them at their various homes. When she went to stay with Andrew and Debo she would often bring with her the artist Duncan Grant, and the scientist Julian Huxley, much to the delight of the Devonshires and their guests. Mrs Ham, as she was known, called the photograph of herself and Andrew at Lismore, pictured here, 'The Poor Young Man who hopes to marry the Rich Old Widow for her money'.

Mrs Ham kept in touch with Lady Redesdale until the latter's death in 1963, though they saw less of each other after the war as Lady Redesdale moved permanently to the island of Inch Kenneth. There she led an isolated life, but she continued to make trips to London until her final illness, and her family frequently visited her on the island.

Top Mrs Hammersley and Lady Redesdale in 1948

Above right The house on the island of Inch Kenneth

Right Lady Redesdale at Inch Kenneth in 1960

Left Andrew Devonshire and Mrs Violet Hammersley at Lismore, 1952

Chatsworth in Derbyshire

Chatsworth was built for the 1st Duke of Devonshire between 1690 and 1720, to the designs of William Talman, and encased the shell of an Elizabethan house. In 1850 the 6th Duke added the long wing to the left in the photograph, employing Wyattville as architect, and rebuilt the village in the park from designs by Joseph Paxton.

Chatsworth has long been famous as one of the most beautiful houses in England, and it contains an equally famous collection of art and furniture. However, when Debo first saw her future home, her impressions of the house were very different from its illustrious reputation. During the war it had been a girls' school, and when she visited it immediately after, it retained the grim aura of an institution. She describes it as 'sad, dark, cold and dirty. It wasn't like a house at all, but more like a barracks. All the nice things were put away, there were no pictures up and chipboard screens covered most of the walls. It was very depressing'.

Andrew's father, the 10th Duke, died in 1950 and huge death duties had to be paid. After much thought Andrew and Debo decided to move back into Chatsworth. This was a momentous task, as the house had to be done up literally from top to bottom. Seventeen bathrooms had to be put in, all the plumbing reorganized and the house rewired. This and the complete redecoration took seven years, and it was not until 1959 that the family finally moved in.

In 1954 Debo had her portrait painted by Pietro Annigoni. She went every day for a month to sit for him in his studio in Edwardes Square. One day the stove exploded and the room filled with smoke, but fortunately the artist, sitter and portrait escaped unscathed. The artist admired dark-haired women and, realizing this, Debo said, 'I'm sorry about my face, I know it's not what you like.'

With a gesture of resignation Annigoni replied, 'It doesn't matter, it's not your fault.'

The portrait is now at Chatsworth.

Debo being painted by Pietro Annigoni in 1954

Cyril Connolly, the author and critic, was brought to
stay at Lismore in 1958 by a mutual friend, the author
Robert Kee. Connolly came to Ireland intending to
buy a house, and Debo arranged for him to see round
several that were for sale in the neighbourhood.
However, nothing came of this, and she does not think
he was ever very serious in his intention.

Debo enjoys all country pursuits, especially shooting, which she find presents to her a great challenge. Her father-in-law did not allow women to shoot, so she did not take it up until she was thirty, after his death in 1950.

All aspects of horses interest Andrew and Debo, racing in particular. Some of their happiest moments ever were watching Andrew's great race mare, Park Top, carrying his colours to victory. Royal Tan was a special favourite. He won the Grand National in 1954, and was then bought by Aly Khan at the dispersal sale of the horses belonging to J. H. Griffin in 1955. He was third in the 1956 National, after which he was given to Debo to end his days peacefully at Lismore.

The family go to Lismore Castle in Ireland each spring for a few weeks. Parts of the castle date back to the reign of King John, and it has been added to in virtually every century since. It came into the Devonshire family through a daughter of Lord Burlington who married Lismore's then owner, Lord Cork. Paxton and the Bachelor (6th) Duke rebuilt and altered large parts of it in the nineteenth century, and Auguste Pugin was responsible for much of the interior, which closely resembles his work at the House of Lords and the House of Commons.

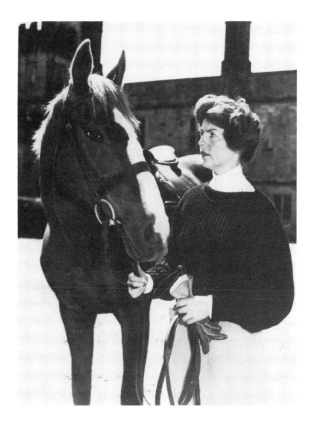

Left Debo out shooting in the park at Chatsworth

Above Debo with Royal Tan in 1958

Below Lismore Castle, Co. Waterford

A LAMENT

FOR
MOIRA McCAVENDISH

BY

"Coras Iompair Eireann"

———◆———

Through the Midlands of Ireland I journeyed by diesel,
    And bright in the sun shone the emerald plain ;
Though loud sang the birds on the thorn-bush and teasel,
    They could not be heard for the sound of the train.

The roll of the railway made musing creative :
    I thought of the Colleen I soon was to see
With her wiry black hair and grey eyes of the native,
    Sweet MOIRA McCAVENDISH, acushla machree.

Her brother's wee cabin stands distant from *Tallow*
    A league and a half, where the *Blackwater* flows,
And the musk and potato, the mint and the mallow
    Do grow there in beauty, along with the rose.

'Twas smoothly we raced through the open expansion
    Of rush-covered levels and gate-lodge and gate
And the ruined demesne and the windowless mansion
    Where once the oppressor had revelled in state.

At *Castletownroche*, as the prospect grew hillier
    I saw the far mountains to MOIRA long-known
'Till I came to the valley and townland familiar
    With the *Protestant* church standing locked and alone.

O vein of my heart ! upon *Tallow Road Station*
    No face was to greet me so freckled and white ;
As the diesel slid out, leaving still desolation,
    The McCAVENDISH ass cart was no where in sight.

For a league and half to the *Blackwater* river
    I tramped with my bundle her cabin to see
And herself by the fuchsias, her young lips a-quiver,
    Half smiling, half weeping a welcome to me.

Och MOIRA McCAVENDISH ! the fangs of the creeper
    Have struck at the thatch and trust open the door ;
The couch in the garden grows ranker and deeper
    Than musk and potato which bloomed there before.

Flow on, you remorseless and salmon-full waters !
    What care I for prospects so silvery fair ;
The heart in me's dead, like your sweetest of daughters,
    And I would that my spirit were lost on the air.

Dedicated by permission to Their Graces

THE DUKE & DUCHESS OF DEVONSHIRE,

The Marquis of Hartington and The Ladies

EMMA AND SOPHIA CAVENDISH.

Browne, Printer, Lismore,

Poem about Lismore by John Betjeman

Debo with Sophia at her christening in 1957. Behind are Emma, Andrew and Peregrine

Sophia was born on 18 March 1957, the youngest by a long way of Debo's three children: Emma, born in 1942, was fourteen when her sister was born, and Peregrine thirteen. The christening took place at the church at Edensor, the village in the park at Chatsworth.

John Betjeman was an old friend of Debo, who had known him since she was nine. In his youth he was a constant visitor to Biddesden, and a great admirer of Pam's. Later he became close friends with Lady Elizabeth Cavendish, Andrew's sister, and so used to see a lot of the Devonshires. For many years he paid an annual visit to Lismore and wrote this poem during one of his stays.

Left Nancy in Paris in 1952

Above Colonel Gaston Palewski

Left Printed card sent by Nancy to acknowledge letters and requests which she did not consider deserved a proper reply

The 1940s and early 1950s were for Nancy perhaps the happiest years in what was overall an unhappy life. What made it sad was that no one ever reciprocated her love to the same extent. Hamish St Clair Erskine, her first love, was gay. With Peter Rodd, disillusionment quickly set in. Nancy was very private and introverted about her feelings and never completely confided in anyone. However, the failure of her marriage probably caused her more pain than she ever admitted to.

The real love of her life was Gaston Palewski, whom she met in England towards the end of the war. Known as 'the Colonel', he was a leading member of de Gaulle's party and fought bravely for the Resistance during the war. Fabrice de Sauveterre in *The Pursuit of Love* and Charles Edouard in *The Blessing* are based on him. Although Palewski returned her affections for a while, he had many other affairs and really regarded her as a great friend and wonderful companion. Their affair came eventually to an end, but they remained on quite good terms. He married towards the end of the 1960s and, curiously enough, it was on the day of his wedding that Nancy felt the first

twinges of the pain of the cancer that was eventually to kill her. There was another strange coincidence. When she was dying, the Colonel suddenly had an urge to see her. He was the last person to see her alive, as she died shortly after he left.

Because of the Colonel, Nancy moved to Paris in 1946, where she borrowed or rented flats until she found a permanent home at No. 7 rue Monsieur. In France, Nancy became an ardent Francophile, loving all things French and despising all things English. When she returned to Paris after a visit to England, she would say, 'When I left Dover it was freezing cold and pouring with rain, and then, suddenly, halfway across the Channel, with France in sight, the clouds would part and out came the sun.'

These feelings were understandable. England held largely unhappy memories for her, whereas living in France she had found success as an authoress and happiness in love. However, she remained an essentially English person. Charles Ritchie, who knew her at this time, described her as a 'queer mixture of county and sophistication – you never know which reaction you are going to strike'.

Nancy's apartment in the rue Monsieur was already partially furnished with some good eighteenth-century pieces when she moved in, to which she added some of her own things from England, and some new acquisitions bought with the proceeds of *The Pursuit of Love* which had been published in 1945. 'I write in the hope of amusing the public and making money for myself' was Nancy's comment on the subject of her writing. With *The Pursuit of Love* she achieved both aspirations. Funny, touching and sad, it immediately became a bestseller and has remained in print ever since.

Many of the characters and scenes are based on her family and childhood; indeed, Lord Redesdale is best known for being the model for Uncle Matthew. Several of the characters reappeared in her next novel, *Love in a Cold Climate*. This was followed by *The Blessing* and, finally in 1961, *Don't Tell Alfred*.

Encouraged by the success of her novels, Nancy turned her attention to historical biography. *Madame de Pompadour* was the first of these, published in 1953, then came *Voltaire in Love*, followed by *The Sun King*, an account of Louis XIV at Versailles, and finally her last book, *Frederick the Great*. These, apart from

being thoroughly researched and historically accurate, were eminently readable. Nancy's eye for detail and sense of humour were as effective here as with her novels, and she had the great talent for bringing her subjects to life.

In 1956 Nancy edited *Noblesse Oblige*, and many people consider it a great pity that Nancy was responsible for this. It came about after she read an article in *Encounter* by Alan Ross, a professor of language who had made a study of different words and expressions used by the so-called upper and middle classes to describe the same thing. He had coined the phrase 'U' and 'Non U' to distinguish the differences. Nancy was highly amused by this, and with the help of Ross and contributions from Evelyn Waugh, John Betjeman and Christopher Sykes, she produced *Noblesse Oblige*. It provoked a lot of people, always the intention of Nancy's teases, and caused quite a stir when it was published. As a result it is almost always this lightweight book which is cited as an example of her work rather than her novels and historical biographies which are far greater achievements.

Cover of *The Pursuit of Love*

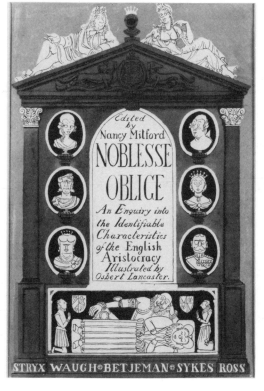

Cover of *Noblesse Oblige*

Nancy at her home in rue Monsieur

This photograph shows the last gathering of the
Mitford sisters, with the exception of Decca. Nancy
was at this time writing her last book, a biography of
Frederick the Great. While she was working on this,
she began to suffer from spasmodic pains in her back
and legs, which gradually got worse and more
frequent. She went to many doctors and specialists, all
of whom came up with different diagnoses and
treatments, but it was finally discovered that she was
suffering from Hodgkin's Disease, a form of
leukaemia which killed her in 1973.

Pam was dividing her time between her house in the
Cotswolds and Switzerland, where she had a half
share in a house near Zurich.

Diana in 1967 was living a happy, uxorious
existence in France. Although she had translated
several books from German and French into English,
she had not yet published anything herself, and was
not to do so until 1977 when her autobiography, *A Life
of Contrasts*, was published. This was followed by a
biography of the Duchess of Windsor and, most
recently, *Loved Ones*, a collection of her memories of
some of her closest friends.

Debo was busy running Chatsworth, attending to

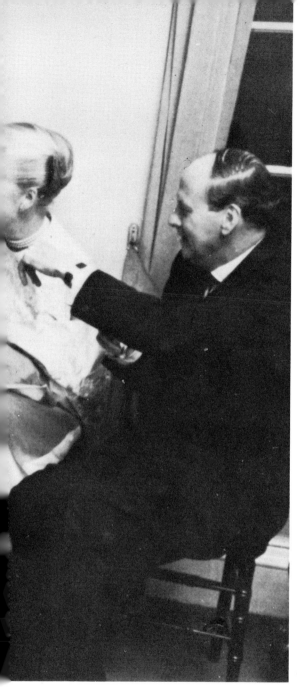

The cast and programme of *The Mitford Girls*, a light-hearted musical produced by Caryl Brahms and Ned Sherrin, based on the lives of the sisters

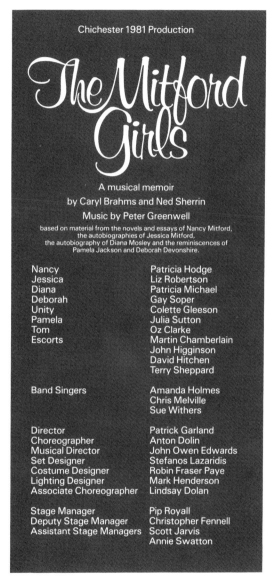

Chichester 1981 Production

The Mitford Girls

A musical memoir
by Caryl Brahms and Ned Sherrin
Music by Peter Greenwell
based on material from the novels and essays of Nancy Mitford,
the autobiographies of Jessica Mitford,
the autobiography of Diana Mosley and the reminiscences of
Pamela Jackson and Deborah Devonshire.

Nancy	Patricia Hodge
Jessica	Liz Robertson
Diana	Patricia Michael
Deborah	Gay Soper
Unity	Colette Gleeson
Pamela	Julia Sutton
Tom	Oz Clarke
Escorts	Martin Chamberlain
	John Higginson
	David Hitchen
	Terry Sheppard
Band Singers	Amanda Holmes
	Chris Melville
	Sue Withers
Director	Patrick Garland
Choreographer	Anton Dolin
Musical Director	John Owen Edwards
Set Designer	Stefanos Lazaridis
Costume Designer	Robin Fraser Paye
Lighting Designer	Mark Henderson
Associate Choreographer	Lindsay Dolan
Stage Manager	Pip Royall
Deputy Stage Manager	Christopher Fennell
Assistant Stage Managers	Scott Jarvis
	Annie Swatton

the million and one tasks that befall inhabitants of stately homes. She had by now become a workaholic. The author can never remember in twenty-eight years of her life seeing her mother relaxing or sitting idle.

…eft to right: Cecil Beaton, Nancy, Debo, Pam, Diana and Andrew …Devonshire at the dance after the wedding of Debo's son Peregrine …artington to Amanda Heywood Lonsdale in 1967

Les admirateurs de l'œuvre de Nancy MITFORD
vous prient d'assister à l'inauguration de la plaque apposée
sur l'immeuble · 4, rue d'Artois, à Versailles · où vécut cette
très grande amie de la France, dont les ouvrages littéraires
et le dévouement à la cause des alliés en 1939-45 font honneur
à la Grande-Bretagne et à notre pays.

MERCREDI 12 JUIN 1974, à 16 h 30

A l'issue de la cérémonie, les sœurs de Nancy Mitford seraient heureuses de vous recevoir pour le thé au Trianon Palace Hôtel, 1 Boulevard de la Reine, à Versailles.

Above The invitation to the ceremony

Below Harold Acton giving the address at the erection of a commemorative plaque to Nancy at 4, rue d'Artois, June 1974

Nancy died in her house in rue d'Artois in Versailles on 30 June 1973. She was cremated in France, but her funeral service was held in the church at Swinbrook where the family used to attend services as children. She was greatly mourned by her family and friends, but her death was a blessed relief from the agonizing illness from which she had suffered for the past four years.

At his request, Nancy's sisters agreed that Sir Harold Acton should write her biography. He had been a lifelong friend and correspondent of Nancy's and her sisters, and had written a number of distinguished books, including his autobiography, *Memoirs of an Aesthete*. He was the ideal candidate for the task, and two years later produced *Nancy Mitford, a Memoir*, a delightful tribute to his old friend. Nancy herself had planned to write her memoirs after she had finished *Frederick the Great*, but she had by then become too ill to carry out the project.

A year after her death a commemorative plaque was put up at her house in Versailles. The ceremony at which Harold Acton read the address was attended by many of her friends and admirers.

Diana, Pamela and Debo at Nancy's funeral, 8 July 1973

Deborah Devonshire, 1985   Pamela Jackson, 1985

For Debo, running Chatsworth is a full-time job. Big estates nowadays have to pay their way, and the Duke and Duchess have constantly to come up with ways to meet the ever-rising costs of keeping afloat the house and estate. Among other projects Debo, with the help of interior designer David Mlinaric, has started a garden furniture business which is now thriving. As a result in the last couple of years they have been able to take on more employees rather than making dreaded redundancies. Debo also acts as a non-executive director of the building firm Tarmac, which she loves, partly no doubt because it is something completely different from her work at Chatsworth.

Debo is a fervent letter writer, writing to each of her sisters at least twice a week, and dealing with all her correspondence and business matters herself. In her bedroom and sitting room are baskets overflowing with accounts, architectural plans, wallpaper samples, horse pedigrees, cuttings from magazines and all manner of letters ranging from charity appeals to comments and criticisms on the use of English from the writer Paddy Leigh Fermor.

Despite the ever-increasing piles of paper, she manages to run her busy life extremely well, yet without a trace of the headmistressy bossiness that so often accompanies good organization. She finds the interest shown in her family incomprehensible, and fights shy of publicity as a Mitford, unless the publicity can be of benefit to Chatsworth. When questioned on the Mitfords, she roars with laughter and says, 'It's all too silly for words'.

Pam, like Debo, responds in similar vein when the question is put, 'Why do you think your family has aroused such interest?'. 'Oh darling, I really don't know,' she replies, 'Oh dear, no, I really can't imagine'. She lives in a village in Gloucestershire, twenty miles from her childhood home at Swinbrook, and her animals, garden and cooking are her main preoccupations.

Since Sir Oswald Mosley's death in 1980 Diana has been able to spend more time visiting her sisters and children in England, but she loves France too much now to contemplate moving back permanently. Her close and loving relationships with all her family are a wonderful comfort and support to her but, after forty-four such happy years with her husband, his death has naturally left a void which can never be filled by others.

Diana Mosley, 1985